Foruli Codex

GLEN MATLOCK'S SEX PISTOLS FILTHY LUCRE PHOTO FILE

Published by Foruli Codex

FIRST EDITION

ISBN 978-1-905792-47-4

Volume copyright © Foruli Ltd 2014
Cover design copyright © Foruli Ltd 2014
Foreword copyright © Chad Smith 2014
Text copyright © Glen Matlock and Joel McIver 2014

Edited by Karl French

Photographs on pages 14, 15, 33, 46, 47, 48, 49, 50, 51, 61, 64, 65, 66, 67, 74, 75, 90, 91, 100, 101, 138, 139, 145, 151 © Foruli Ltd / Andy Vella

All items of memorabilia, press clippings and ephemera are from Glen Matlock's personal archives

Every effort has been made to trace and acknowledge the respective copyright holders. We apologise in advance for any unintentional omissions and would be pleased, if any such case should arise, to add appropriate acknowledgment in any future edition of the book.

The right of Glen Matlock and Joel McIver to be identified as the author of this work has been asserted by them in accordance with the Copyright, Designs and Patents Act 1988.

All rights reserved. No part of this publication may be reproduced, stored in or introduced into a retrieval system, or transmitted, in any form or by any means (electronic, mechanical, photocopying, recording or otherwise), without the prior written permission of the publisher. This book is sold subject to the condition that it shall not, by way of trade or otherwise, be lent, re-sold, hired out, or otherwise circulated without the publisher's prior written consent in any form of binding or cover other than that in which it is published and without a similar condition including this condition being imposed on the subsequent purchaser.

A CIP catalogue record for this book is available from the British Library

Design by Andy Vella at Velladesign, www.velladesign.com

Typeset in Palatino

Printed by Lightning Source

Foruli Codex is an imprint of Foruli Ltd, London

www.forulicodex.com

CONTENTS

FOREWORD
INTRODUCTION
EUROPE
NORTH AMERICA
AUSTRALASIA
JAPAN
SOUTH AMERICA
EPILOGUE 146

FOREWORD	7
INTRODUCTION	8
EUROPE	39
NORTH AMERICA	71
AUSTRALASIA	83
JAPAN	93
SOUTH AMERICA	135

(WORD)

I was only barely aware of the Sex Pistols in the late '70s and I certainly never saw them on their "original" post-Matlock, American tour (of course a lot of people say they saw that tour - we call those people "fucking liars"). At the time I was 17 years old and way too busy rocking out to the very bands Glen and company were supposedly rebelling against. It wasn't until I joined the Peppers that I began to appreciate what the Pistols had done to rock and roll. In typical Brit fashion, they threw it up against the wall, spat on it, gave it the middle finger, and sold it to us Yanks, just like the Stones and The Who had done 15 years earlier, when they were still sneering punks. I could get behind that.

Fast forward the VHS to 1996 and I'm standing at the Palladium watching the reformed Pistols onstage. Squint your eyes and it almost looks like Jonesy fits into his snakeskin pants. Close your eyes and it sounds like 1977. The energy, the attitude, the sweat - you can't fake that shit. They may not have been the best of friends, but when they hit that first chord they were as compelling as a gunshot. The filth and the fury, it was all there.

I've always thought that being in a band is like being married to three other people, only without the sleeping together part. In Glen's case, those three other people happened to be Johnny Rotten, Steve Jones and Paul Cook. The Pistols didn't last very long, but they left a mark on music and they've influenced a lot of bands, including the Peppers. Gluttons for punishment that they are, in 1996 the band decided to have another go at it. Here's Glen's account of the Filthy Lucre tour, warts and all. It's hilarious, scary, thrilling and ugly, all at the same time, just like the band itself.

Before you start reading, you might want to buy some hand-sanitizer just to be safe. In the case of the Pistols, rock and roll is a communicable disease.

Enjoy the ride...

CHAD SMITH
RED HOT CHILI PEPPERS

INTRODUCTION

Remember 1976 and 1977? I do. The Sex Pistols, who were singer John 'Johnny Rotten' Lydon, guitarist Steve Jones, me on bass and Paul Cook on drums, did a few things that might jog your memory. We did the Bill Grundy Show. Questions were being asked about us in Parliament. We were being put on trial by Fleet Street. The Pistols were quite a handy diversion in the context of the three-day week, power cuts and a hung parliament. We took the heat off what the government were doing at the time, and we did it by speaking our minds. That was the whole Sex Pistols ethos.

There had a been a couple of suggestions over the years that we should reform the band, but nothing happened until I went to Los Angeles in 1995 and met Steve. It was never on the cards before that. I'd say it was either Steve or me who started the reunion off. This is how it happened.

In 1995, I went to America to work on a project with the producer Mickie Most. I went over with Steve New from the Rich Kids to meet a singer: he was a lovely bloke and very interesting, but he wasn't much of a singer. Mickie's son Calvin Hayes was putting me up at his place in West Hollywood, and after a few rehearsals I said, 'This isn't really working out, Calvin.' He said 'Why don't you hang on for a bit longer?' so I said, 'Do you know what, I haven't spoken to Steve Jones in 17 years and I know he's over here. I fancy catching up with him.'

Next day Calvin said, 'I've got Steve's number here, why don't you give him a call?' but I said, 'Hmm...' because a lot of shit had been said over the years that I thought was below the belt and unnecessary. So I wasn't in a rush to call him, but Calvin came back and said, 'Have you called Steve?' and I said 'Nah'. He said 'Call him!' I was in a bit of a quandary, because I'd written as much, if not more, of the Sex Pistols' songs than the other guys, and then they'd said that horrible shit about me when they didn't need to.

This went on for about three or four days. In the end I called Steve and he said, 'Oh hello, I heard you was around, do you want to go to a party at Pamela Des Barres' house?' I said yes and went down there to meet him. When I arrived, I didn't know anybody there, and Pamela said to me, 'Can I help you?' I said, 'I'm looking for Steve Jones' and she said 'Oh, you must be Glen!' I met Steve and we got chatting, and he said, 'Shall we go and see John?' I said, 'When?' and he said, 'Tomorrow'. I said, 'OK then,' and the next day we went and met John at his place in Venice. It was a bit odd at first, but we got on all right. Then Steve said, 'Let's call Paul.' He was really pushing for us all to meet. We called Paul in England, but he wasn't in, so we left a message and met up with him when we got back.

The first time I met John again, there was all sorts of stuff going through my mind, just as I'm sure there was stuff going through his. We arrived at his house and I went to the loo. He came downstairs and we literally bumped into each other, which defused the tension. It was fine. He told me about the album he was making at the time and that he was playing the keyboards on it. I asked him how many fingers he was using.

We went out and he had a good drink. I dropped him back at his place and there was a walkway going down to where he lived, and the Pacific ocean was on either side of the walkway. John was zigzagging all the way down it and I got out of the car and made sure he didn't fall in. He was saying, 'Glen, you're being so nice to me, even after all the things I said about you!' and I said, 'Well, we've got a tour to do, John'.

After that, it made sense to play together again. Funny how so much of the reunion was driven by meetings in America, considering that we were supposed to be a British band.

We hired a manager, a woman called Anita Camarata who'd been sorting out the Pistols' back catalogue, and some feelers were put out. At the end of 1995 a world tour started coming together. It was very exciting, but I was wary: we got on well, generally, but what had been said in the press was alluded to a couple of times. I made a point of hanging out with John every now and then, because to me, there had always been a triumvirate in the Sex Pistols. There was John; there was me; and then there was Steve and Paul together, who make up a kind of double act.

The dynamic between us was the way it had always been in the old days. The way Steve works is that he does the gig and he's off, mainly because if you've given up booze, you don't want to be around people who are doing stuff. I'm sure every band is like that to different degrees, but in the Sex Pistols you've got some larger-than-life characters.

The first thing was to hold a press conference, and this we did on March 16, 1996 at the 100 Club in London.

The press just treated us as something else to write about. The media need things to fill pages and TV shows, every day of the week, and when the Sex Pistols reform you've done that job for them. So why they were so generally miserable about it, I'm not sure. John was good at that kind of thing: when someone said, 'Why are you doing this for the money?' and he said 'Yes, we've come for your money,' I liked that. When he said that we were 'fat, forty and back,' he added 'I've always been forty,' and it's true, he has.

Now, at the time I had a solo album called *My Little Philistine* coming out on the Creation label. I'd met the label owner Alan McGee the previous year, and he'd said, 'What are you up to?' and I said, 'I've got a load of songs and I'm thinking about making a record.' I'd been through the whole thought process of 'What am I doing with my life? Nothing's happening. I got pissed a lot and ended up with a drink problem, so I stopped drinking. What am I going to do now?' and I was getting back into writing music. So McGee said, 'All right, I'll put the record out,' and we started recording it. It was finished and supposed to come out in January 1996, but it got pushed back for a couple of reasons and then the Pistols thing happened. I had gigs booked, but the record kept being put back, so I had to keep cancelling them. I think McGee thought it was cool to put it out at the same time as the Pistols tour, but I didn't think it was.

I'd done the Creation album before there was even any talk of the Pistols reforming. It got buried by it. I wanted it to come out earlier in 1996 but it got held up for some technical reason, and then they hung onto it when the Pistols came together. They thought it would be a good idea to coincide it with the Pistols, and I didn't – and when it came out it looked like I was cashing in with it. But I wrote those songs in 1994 and recorded them in 1995. I think it's a good album. Over the past 15 years I've written four good albums, actually. I think some people are beginning to understand that I was an important songwriter in the band, but it looks like 'Pretty Vacant' will always be the song I'm best known for.

I never gave up. There's not a lot you can do about the way the music industry works, and I was always making new music, even if wasn't always successful. When John said 'Nothing,' after someone asked me at the press conference what I'd been doing for the last 20 years, I thought it was unreasonable since I had an album out on Creation. I nipped that kind of talk in the bud.

I do have a sense of humour, and I laughed when John was making his jokes, but I didn't really go much on him calling Lady Diana the 'Queen Of Tarts'. Both me and Paul, who live in England, thought it was a bit facile and naff. She was just an easy target. She died while I was in Paris the following year, actually: I was in the city at the time, although it wasn't my fault...

I didn't know this until he told me afterwards, but Steve drank a bottle of Blue Nun to himself a few minutes before the Grundy show. We went in there and they ushered us into the green room. Steve was in there first, and it was winter so we all had big coats on, and he was in and out with something under his coat. We had a rummage through the drinks and me, John and Paul had one of those little 33cl Heineken beers each, and there was nothing else but Steve had come out with the bottle of Blue Nun into the other room and drunk the fucking thing himself. Ten minutes later we're on the telly.

People thought I swore, and I don't really care if I did or not, but I actually didn't. Steve interjected off-camera, 'Fuckin' spank it,' and it looks as if I'm saying it. But it was Steve, because the Blue Nun had kicked in by then. Bill Grundy didn't really clock it properly: he knew something had happened. He asked John something, and John said 'Shit,' trying to cover it up. Grundy made him repeat it: he hadn't been going to say it, originally. Then all hell broke loose. 'Rotter' is the best thing about it.

After the show I went back to the green room to see if they'd restocked the beers, but McLaren said, 'Come on! Now!' and he slung us in the car. Just as we drove away, the Black Maria pulled up and all these coppers jumped out with truncheons. If I'd gone for another drink, I'd have been nicked.

I was living in Chiswick at the time and I got a call from Sophie Richmond, who worked for Malcolm, and she said, 'You've got to come over to Leicester Square for a big meeting.' It took me a little while to get there: I was the last one to arrive – and there were all these photographers waiting for us. I said, 'What's this about?' and Malcolm said, 'You'll find out'.

What had happened was that Queen had pulled out of the show at the last minute, and because they were on EMI, like us, the press guy got us on instead. Bill Grundy didn't really want to interview us. I found out after the event from a bloke who lived around the corner from me who knew Grundy that there had been some shit going on at the TV studio: Bill had said that he didn't want to interview us, not because he didn't like us or anything, just because he didn't know anything about us. There was a bit of a power struggle between him and the producers, who said, 'If you don't interview them, you're out' – two minutes before we were on air. Plus he'd had a drink. He picked on the wrong blokes. That's what it was all about. Someone was looking for a fight with him, and he tried to take it out on us.

SeX PiSTOLS

Aged Sex Pistols rock against the clock

By Nigel Reynolds, Arts Correspondent

THE surviving members of the Sex Pistols, the punk rock band whose utter horribleness excited one generation and appalled several others in the Seventies, gathered in London yesterday to announce that they are to reform for a world tour.

Predictably, they gave a virtuoso display of cynicism and yobbishness, what we look like. We love our beer bellies and you will too."

Sex Pistols — who sold themselves in their heyday as anarchists and anti-stars — should reunite almost 20 years after their last concert, might be seen as a betrayal of their nihilistic principles.

Neatly, the group, whose notoriety overdose after he was charged with murdering his girlfriend Nancy Spungen in New York — refused to disclose how much they would earn from their tour.

At a London press conference Rotten, who now lives in California, Among the critics are Malcolm McLaren, the Seventies style guru who created and managed the Sex Pistols and who subsequently fell out with the group. Describing the reunion plans, he said recently, "They're being sent out like old dray

Still Rotten after all these years...

By SPENCER BRIGHT
at last night's Sex Pistols concert Finsbury Park, London

NINETEEN years ago, they were so feared that councillors banished them from their towns and broadcasters banned them from the airwaves.

Now John Lydon and the reunited Sex Pistols are no more threatening than a Women's Institute meeting in fancy dress.

This fortysomething group of punks had come to snarl and swear and Lydon, once reviled as Johnny Rotten, seemed perturbed by the lukewarm reaction.

With tongue firmly in cheek, he said: "Don't be so shy. It's only Johnny — that, 40 and back."

The group that set out to destroy all heroes produced two of today's biggest to introduce them, though admittedly England footballers Stuart Pearce and Gareth Southgate looked a little embarrassed.

Actor Johnny Depp, model Kate Moss, Oasis stars Liam and Noel Gallagher, as well as a few old punk stars, saw the group arrive on stage tearing through a paper curtain of their notorious tabloid headlines from the Seventies. The music? Well the earth beneath Finsbury Park — which registered on the Richter Scale during a Madness concert a couple of years back — didn't shake.

They started with the song Bodies — riveting on record, but here simply raucous. As they went through their short repertoire — they only produced one album with their original line-up — even Lydon recognised that the response was muted.

But the Pistols, who have dubbed their comeback The Filthy Lucre Tour, are expected to net at least £1million each by the time their world tour is complete.

Punk in the pink: In 1977

IT WAS PRETTY CYN...

SAME OLD JOHNNY, ROTTEN WITH AGE

THE Sex Pistols are back, a lot older, a lot fatter and just as foul-mouthed.

Johnny Rotten and the rest of the band — Glen Matlock, Paul Cook and Steve Jones — had 200 journalists in hysterics at the relaunch of their punk band at London's 100 Club yesterday.

And predictably the middle-aged rockers confessed it was money that prompted their comeback after 20 years.

Q: Is this a proper reunion?

Johnny: Well, Sid Vicious' ashes are scattered over Heathrow .. to have a full reunion we'd need a Hoover.

Q: What do you think of Oasis and the new bands?

Johnny: Trashy little pop stars.

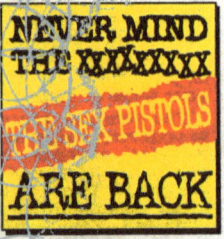

Q: What magazine would you like to appear in?

Johnny: Hello, with Di but not Fergie. She's the Clash of the Royal family.

Q: What about your fans? They're a lot older.

Johnny: I hope it rains at Finsbury Park, so our 'geriatric' fans get their wheelchairs stuck in the mud.

Q: Will there be any rehearsals?

Johnny: No need. It's likely we'll beat the crap out of each other in the first three seconds.

It was pretty cynical at times, the way the press behaved. None of us are stupid, though, and we all realised that there was a game to play. It didn't matter because we all believed in ourselves and we all wanted to make the reunion work - and hopefully we would have a laugh along the way and be a good band, which I think we were. One headline ran 'Antiquity in the UK'... it was all so cheap. My mate Pete Silverton, who was the co-writer of my first book, *I Was A Teenage Sex Pistol*, asked me how it was going, and I said, 'Do you know, Pete, I can't believe the standard of journalism nowadays'. He said, 'It's really hard to find a good plumber and all.'

The journalists were mostly OK, but there was one bloke who was a bit arsey from the *NME*: he said, 'Are you gonna get the sack straight away, Glen?' It might have been just a joke to him, but with what was going on in my head at the time, it wasn't funny at all. I had a real sense of insecurity: a lot of shit had been said, as I explained before. Then again I had to be a part of it, because it wouldn't have been the original band without me, after all. They could have used Duff McKagan of Guns N'Roses or someone instead, which would have been a very LA thing to do, but it wouldn't have been the Sex Pistols.

We look pretty young in this page from the *Sunday Times*. Not many bands had reformed at this stage, which is why we made it into the broadsheets and not just the music magazines. I never sat down and analysed how successful the tour would be, but I did think that it might be a big deal due to the number of people who had come up to me over the years and asked about it.

Someone asked me if playing with the Pistols was like putting on an old comfortable pair of shoes, and I said, 'Yes it is... but with a drawing pin in one of them.'

This time it was for the money, we said: well, when it came to what we earned from the Filthy Lucre tour, there was what we thought we were going to get beforehand, and then there was what we actually got afterwards when everyone had had their slice of it and we'd paid our taxes. We did all right: it was well worth doing, but I'm not telling you how much it was.

The Pistols' old manager Malcolm McLaren said that we were being sent out like old dray horses before being put out to pasture. He felt left out, didn't he? Paul told me a story about Malcolm. When we decided to get back together, Paul called him and said, 'How are you doing, Malcolm? We're going to reform. Do you want to manage us?' Malcolm said, 'Yes please!' and Paul said 'Well, you can't' and put the phone down. I don't know if that story is true, to this day.

FROM PREVIOUS PAGE

Rotten: "Hello, if you give me respect, give these respect, alright? That's it, period. I never ever claimed anything other than these are the original songwriters with me."

Matlock: "Everybody tries to make out that it's some kind of competition between the four of us. And it ain't. We originally got John in the band because he had the gift of the gab, he could put into words what we were thinking. Steve had the great guitar sound, I've got the bass sorted and Paul's a great drummer. That's how bands work. If everybody didn't do their part then you wouldn't have the Pistols. End of story."

Rotten: "Then you wouldn't have had the wonderful original world of modern music. You certainly wouldn't have rap, you wouldn't have gave. You wouldn't have anything at all."

Rap comes from the Sex Pistols. How so?

Rotten: "Rap is a continuation of the Sex Pistols. It's quite obvious. Black kids watched and went, 'Hello, if those white guys can stand up and say they're fed up living in council f—ing flats' then they can be bored with living in the projects."

Matlock: "Lots of things came from punk – reggae coming to the fore, women playing in bands. It was a melting pot."

Glen Matlock getting thrown out of the most dangerous group in the country. That came from punk too. Are you scared it will happen again? Out on your fanny. Jah Wobble brought in before the end of the tour?

Matlock: "I don't think I'll even bother to answer that question."

Jones: "It's in the contract that he has to suck me off once a week. But that's all."

Rotten: "I've already had the threat from Steve – Axl Rose can do what you do."

Jones: "The only problem is he ain't got no hair."

Matlock: "Is he a balding c—?"

Jones: "Yeah, he's lost all his hair, that's why you ain't seen him around."

Rotten (draining his lungs of phlegm, a sound like an industrial vacuum draining a slurry pit): "How brilliant. It's all that patting on the 'ead, ain't it?"

STEVE JONES moved to LA years ago because a bouncer-cum-bodyguard was going to beat him up. "One of my mates," sneers Rotten, gleefully.

Jones: "We ended up in New York and he wanted to kill me because in his weird, coked-up mind he'd get upset because I wouldn't share my girls with him. He said, 'If you get on the plane I'm going to beat you up'. So I've been here ever since."

Rotten (laughing): "Sounds like a professional organisation to me. The bouncer's going to stop my leg. I think I'm going to move to LA. This is all true by the way."

Moving to America was a way out for Jones. When the Pistols split, it hit him hard and he got into smack. This despite having witnessed the Sid and Nancy floorshow wind towards its inevitable conclusion during the Pistols first and, until this year, last American tour: "It was out of boredom, not feeling good about myself. It filled a hole. I was just lost."

Matlock admits to experiencing the same feeling. "When your formative years have been in something as exciting and as big as the Pistols, how else can what happens next be a let-down?"

Cook: "It was very depressing when we split up and the way we split up."

Rotten: "It hurt me no end that, it really did."

Cook: "It's difficult to deal with when you're 21."

Cook and Jones went to Rio with McLaren, making prize prannets of themselves by making records and shooting film with Ronnie Biggs. Did they not feel they'd betrayed Rotten?

Rotten: "No, course not, they'd never feel that. You're asking for the f—ing bloody impossible – trying to make these geezers feel guilty."

Jones: "You know what – later on I did, I felt like I let John down."

Cook: "Yeah, we should have stuck together as a band and f—ed Malcolm."

Jones: "At the time I didn't see that."

Rotten: "But to let you off that, I'd become really unbearably snot-nosed because I was isolated and fed up with it. Destruction was all I'd seen around me and I really resented that. I wasn't allowed to stay in the same hotels as you, half the gaffs I was chucked into didn't have phones, come-ridden f—ing pillows…"

The tour wasn't much fun either.

Cook: "It was f—ing horrible, it really finished us off."

Jones: "It was Barnum and Bailey, know what I mean?"

Rotten: "Roll up and join the fun, sing along the circus is in town tra la la. It was sooooo bad. Sid onstage going flumpf flumpf. Paul and Steve couldn't bear me at that point. Tried to repair it. one night Steve and me met. Remember?

"We had a shoebox full of hash and just giggled and then it was all over because within two hours the police were called. Sid was found with a black transvestite in the hotel and it was just nonsense and it just went on and on and on in the most silly, stupidest drug-induced way."

But couldn't it all have been so different? Why did they ever get that loser Sidney in the band, why not just carry on hating Matlock?

Rotten: "That's down to politics, we've talked about this since. The fings I was led to believe about Glen, and I'm sure Glen was led to believe things about me, ultimately both of us don't take responsibility for. Somebody told us a f—ing crock of shit and it was nasty, evil, spiteful, vindictive and manipulative."

Matlock: "Malcolm's whole game was to divide and conquer and he did anything he could to perpetrate that basically."

And yet Matlock, still nicknamed Albert after Albert Tatlock, an aged uptight '70s cornerstone of Coronation Street, stayed friends with Vicious, a near-neighbour in Maida Vale. He even joined Vicious White Kids, the band Sid put together for his last ever appearance on a London stage.

Matlock: "I can't understand how he had a gig in the best band in the world and still f—ing blew it. I remember when we were rehearsing that Vicious White Kids gig he said to me, 'Glen, how can you play bass the whole way through a song without stopping?'"

SO TO the good stuff, the music. 'God Save The Queen,' Lydon remembers as "a bunch of bitterness", scribbled early one morning on his mother's kitchen table. The song became an alternative national anthem when it became a 'banned' Number One in Jubilee week, though it should have been released months earlier when A&M withdrew it from circulation.

Rotten: "That's how the Pistols worked; everyone would have their own little pieces of nastiness working for them. And like all good songs you keep it short, sharp and to the point. And now this is the most difficult aspect for me because I never realised that I wrote so many damned f—ing lyrics. Those songs never end!

"I used to think I was being really specific. Maybe I was, but I had a lot to say and not a lot has changed since. That will be the way always, until the day I die. I'm a big mouth and I like it.

"I'm also incredibly insecure and very, very shy. It's very embarrassing for me to admit but it's the reality of it – that's not a bad thing. These are people I can trust. Do you understand that? We might not like each other but we respect each other in another way that's altogether much more important. No, it ain't no male bonding thing."

Cook: "Anyway, it's one of the greatest fallacies going that bands get on great and it's all buddy buddy on the road."

Some of the strongest objectors to your reformation are original followers who think you've betrayed everything the group stood for.

Rotten: "Anybody who understood us in the first place would understand why we are together now. Anybody who differs from that point of view is a pretend fan, a Johnny-come-lately who is faking it." (Sings), 'Don't fake it baby, lay the real thing on me'."

Most recently employed as Edwyn Collins' drummer (he plans to work with him again in the autumn) Paul Cook, like Matlock, never left England. He remembers the '80s as "horrible – tossy electro bands thinking they were great". The only time he would be applauded for firing the Pistols battle charge was when he went to football matches.

Rotten: "That's so f—ing right. The only people that really understood anarchy were football hooligans."

Jones: "And when you went down to the public lavs in Piccadilly Circus they'd say, 'You're one of them Sex Pistols. Prove it to me. Prove it.'"

Jones says he'll spend all his money from the Filthy Lucre tour on prostitutes. Later during dinner Rotten says of Jones, "I respect that guy more than anyone. I respect anyone who makes a big change. Steve just said no. He gave up drugs for sex, which is what he's good at. I love him, I know he feels the same about me, though he'd never say it."

Jones' solo career amounted to two albums, since then he's earned his stripes as a jobbing LA musician. Over the years he's recorded with Guns N'Roses, Iggy Pop and Bob Dylan ("I went down, played a song, then another and another. It was a lot of shit really"). But the best thing he's done outside of the Pistols is, he says, an unreleased song written and recorded with the late Roy Orbison.

"You don't do a solo career to make money. Anyone who's in a big band and goes solo just sells ten copies, you only do it for your own ego."

How do you view your solo career now?

Jones: "I don't really. I just wanted to get something out of me. If you think you can write songs and you don't get it out I think it turns into f—ing cancer."

Now they are back together. The Pistols, once so different, are like every other rock institution,

Anarchy in LA 1996 (l-r): Matlock, Cook, Rotten and Jones

cashing in their pension plan. Cook says that "at least we haven't been boring the arse off everyone like The Who or The Rolling Stones for the past 20 years". When he adds that they aren't really making much money from the tour, not compared with The Eagles, Rotten becomes inflamed. "Paul, don't ever apologise for yourself, there's no need to do that."

Rotten admits he "ran away from it (the reunion) for a long time". An instinct for self-preservation?

Rotten: "In a way, but mostly because everybody had their bit to say about it. They scandalised it and rewrote history to suit themselves. I began to resent people rewriting my history for me, telling me what I originally thought about things. That pissed me off. I put a book out (No Blacks, No Dogs, No Irish, his fascinating autobiography) to clean it up. Once I did that I felt a hellvalot better. That cleaned my mind. I don't have the same problems as ten years ago. People like Malcolm saying he did this and he did that really offended and upset me. We weren't communicating at all during that period. I'd run into Paul every now and then. It was bad to run into each other, very difficult.

"Maybe time mellows things out in that respect. But it certainly hasn't mellowed out the content. Rehearsing the last two days, my God, we're so f—ing the same way. It's delicious, we're at war. We're playing against each other but the songs work. Everyone is trying to f— you up. It's NICE!

"They are simple enough songs, we know that. But they're tricky dicky; they have little bombs waiting for you. In the end, that's the stuff. Maybe that's why people can't play them, only we can."

Despite living in LA with his wife Nora, purportedly a very wealthy German heiress, Rotten says his ardour has not weakened.

"I'm angry and I'm going to be angry all my life. I was born and raised that way and told I had no opportunity at every turn. It's an outrage to me that you can make a lot of money and then why you're great but I still can't get into any of those posh clubs in London. I wanna know what's going on. Why can't I be in there like everybody f—ing else, what makes one person more important than another?"

There's vague talk about new songs being written but Rotten thinks the tour may finish the Pistols' collective and solo careers off once and for all. There's a mix of bravado and nerves behind the statement – it could be glorious, it could be disastrous. It could be a f— you farewell, a no future finale, a rock'n'roll wake.

Rotten: "Only if you're from southern Ireland. Hello, my mum died. I celebrated her funeral in the best way possible. I wrote 'Death Disco' for my mum. I played it to her before she died while she was sprawled on a hospital bed, riddled with cancer. It was important for me that she would appreciate it and she did. She thought it was hilarious. That's my way, my family's way but that's not everybody's way."

And the tour?

Rotten: "Same thing possibly, it would be a delicious metaphor. Goodbye mummy."

Cook: "Goodbye Pistols."

You want to destroy your legacy?

Rotten: "I hope that is exactly what we're doing. That is the point, people have built this up into being something it ain't. You must not treat us as gods, just, hello, a job well done. Thank you; that's good enough. If I walk out to a hall of boos it won't be that different to what I'm used to in this band in the first place. Except it can't ever be as violent and hateful as it was. Or maybe it can be. Who knows? (Sings) 'I've got to solve that mystery baby.'"

An odd mix of contrary bastard and brutally honest beast, Rotten says it's the other three who are doing him a favour by going back on the road. If he wants to destroy the Sex Pistols' myth and mystery once and for all he needs their support as much, maybe more, than they need his.

Outside the restaurant, the support is literal. Johnny Rotten, an Anglo-Irish man in LA, charming dinner date and supreme wind-up merchant, wraps his rubber coat around his billowing ripped and ragged clothes. There are no farewells. He shrugs his shoulders, focuses his eyes, debilitated by severe meningitis in childhood, flooded with drink tonight. He walks towards the waiting Matlock who puts his arm around him. Off he goes, just like he sang all those years ago at the end of 'Anarchy In The UK', pissed and ready to destroy.

CRADLE
(featuring TERRY BICKERS)

the debut single
SECOND NATURE
out now

7-inch vinyl/CD single (4 tracks)

COMING SOON: THE ALBUM: BABA YAGA

ultimate

DISTRIBUTED BY pinnacle

I'm not sure whose ideas the tart cards were, but we had one each: they tied in with the Filthy Lucre concept. This is a photo of of me passed out somewhere, who knows where? Jack Daniel's whiskey was my poison of choice back in the early days.

Open 36 hours only
http://www.sexpistols.com
http://www.hob.com/sexpistols

LUXUR
LET'S CO

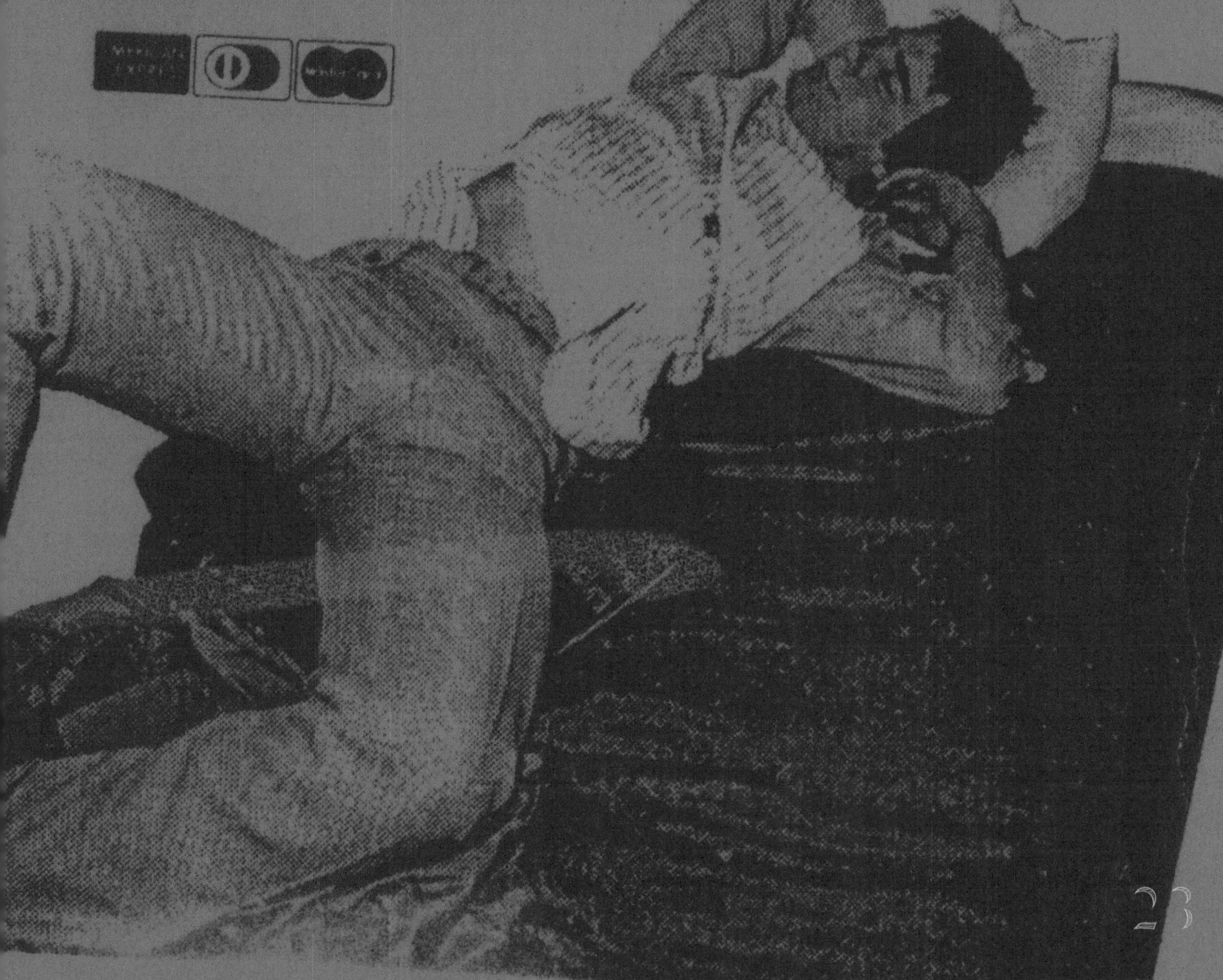

Proving Malcolm wrong was one element of our motivation, but it wasn't the whole reason for doing it. He'd pretended that we were his puppets, and that he'd created us and that we were nothing without him, which was all untrue. We were claiming it back for ourselves, while getting paid and even better, getting paid without giving a slice of it to Malcolm, which must have hurt him, because he didn't get a penny from the Pistols. John took him to court after he used the royalties to make *The Great Rock'N'Roll Swindle*, and John was quite rightly annoyed about that, because it's just wrong to have money used for that reason without being asked. There was no verdict, because Malcolm retired from the case when he was going to lose and he couldn't afford to pay the costs. We were freed up to do a lot more things after that, because all the money was held in escrow by the lawyers. Nobody was dragging us out on tour: we were doing it of our own volition, so when Malcolm said that about dray horses, we just thought, 'The poor old fucker, he's jealous'.

I last saw Malcolm when I was in the States in 2009. I hadn't spoken to him for years, although I'd seen him about five years before that in a little restaurant around the corner from where I live. He was in the window of the restaurant, obviously freeloading a meal off some people. You only had to look and you could see what was going on. Anyway, I was walking down University Place in New York in '09 and it was a gorgeous sunny day. Lo and behold, there's Malcolm coming down the street towards me with a girl who was holding a clipboard: she looked like some sort of intern from the University, but it transpired that she was his partner. Anyway, he didn't see me, so I said, 'Hello, Malcolm, how are you doing?' and he went, 'Oh! Matlock! What are you doing here? You're looking good! Um... Er...' and backed off. Maybe he thought I was going to land him one. And then a few months later I heard he was really ill.

I really didn't know what to think when I heard of his death in April 2010: I loved Malcolm when I first met him. I thought he was great, and a real pleasure to be with. But you have to remember that he sent a telegram to the NME in 1977 saying that I'd been sacked for liking the Beatles, and that was after he'd demanded a meeting, saying, 'Glen, I've made a big mistake, I think you should be the bass player, Sid Vicious is rubbish, blah blah, will you reconsider?' I said, 'Malcolm, don't. You played me wrong,' and we shook hands on it. That cost me millions of pounds, if you think about it. I went to his funeral and I still don't know what to think. It was a very symbiotic relationship: without Malcolm, no-one would ever have heard of the Sex Pistols, and without the Sex Pistols, no-one would ever have heard of Malcolm McLaren.

MUSIC

Pistols Return to Rewrite History

Punk pioneers claim reunion is less about money than proving Malcolm McLaren wrong

BY SHAWN CONNER

Imagine it's 1976, and the charts are ruled by Boston, Kansas, Styx, and REO Speedwagon. Sounds like a nightmare, doesn't it? But it really happened. Then imagine the same charts circa 1977, after the Sex Pistols burst onto the English music scene: Boston, Kansas, Styx, and REO Speedwagon...

Look at the charts today, though, and the Pistols' influence is unmistakable. Would Alice in Chains, the Smashing Pumpkins, No Doubt, Garbage, Soundgarden, or (and you have to take the bad with the good) Bush X exist if not for the Sex Pistols? It may have taken 20 years, but the Pistols have won by attrition.

So it's understandable that some people are upset by the reunion of the most infamous punk band of them all; the Sex Pistols have come to mean a lot of things to a lot of people. Drummer Paul Cook realizes this but makes no apologies. "I knew a lot of people were going to be pissed off about it, because the Pistols have become a bit sacrosanct over the years," says Cook, on the phone from a hotel in Denver, Colorado. "But I didn't like the way

Beneath the anarchic exterior of Sex Pistols drummer Paul Cook (second from left) lurks a proud and oddly professional musician, who hopes his group's reunion tour will lay to rest the myth that the Pistols couldn't play.

Steve's tart card was a beauty. He used to love getting his old chap out anyway, as you might see in some of the other pictures in this book, so it suited him down to the ground. He and I got on really well all through the reunion tour: he was on the wagon like me, and he was heavily into fitness because he was in great shape at the time, so we used to go on power walks together. Some people might not expect stuff like that to happen, but we were grown-up men by this point, so there you go.

GOLDEN SHOWERS

Here's a caricature of us, with Steve looking fat. That's not cool: Steve was in great shape. They've written 'Not so Vicious' on my T-shirt. They could have written 'Damn fine bass player who wrote a lot of good tunes', but that was never likely to happen, was it?

We appeared on the cover of *MOJO*. People complained because we weren't wearing bondage trousers, 20 years after the event. I think we looked rather good in our designer suits. In retrospect, it didn't feel that the press were out to get us, particularly: it was a game that we were playing in their studenty minds. As long as we were getting the column inches, it was all right with us. I remember one magazine didn't give us the cover and all hell broke loose.

Mind you, there were a few herberts. Some of the press could be a bit arsey. But they were normally the people who didn't know what the fuck I had actually done to make it work. John understands how the press works far more than I do, not that I don't understand it at all, but he was good at playing the game.

Here's Steve saying that he was a genius and that he started punk. Nobody picked up that we all said, to a man, 'I did it all! It was me!' Steve knew how to play the game when getting grilled by the press, just like the rest of us. Most of the journalists were on our side, but there were always one or two who wanted to stick the knife in and twist it a bit.

MUSIC

Pistol whipped

eye's two-page special on the Filthy Lucre tour by the original toothless punks kicks off with Sex Pistols guitarist Steve Jones speaking his, er, mind

CINDY McGLYNN

Isn't it ironic, you think, quoting the timeless words of Alanis (which I like to do whenever I get the chance), that punk's original bad boys are back almost two decades later? They're singing a new tune, although not any new songs — insisting out one side of their mouths that the songs matter as much as ever. And out of the other side spewing, and I quote, "I don't give a shit. Just give me your fuckin' money."

"Uh, no, no really," is the answer you come up with. Because you just remembered that the Sex Pistols were a bunch of loud-mouth, street-smart, skanky London louts. That they would've been as pleased as anyone with half a brain to take the money back then, if Uncle Malcolm would've let them. And that it probably took 'em 18 years just to figure out how to fuckin' spell 'reunion.' Nevertheless, I find this little exercise oddly compelling despite, or maybe because of, its pointlessness. And so… *Oi!* rock kids — close your eyes and think of England, we're gonna have a chat with a Sex Pistol!

To set the tone I'd like you to imagine a crackly conference line with you, Sex Pistol Steve Jones, a publicist and a small beast yelping for its fuckin' life. (You have to swear a lot when you talk about the Sex Pistols.)

"Go and strangle that bleedin' dog," Steve says. "It's on the third-party line. I have a dog, but it's really quiet."

Versa, the publicist: "It's not my dog, it's the neighbor's dog."

Me: "Um. Is Mr. Jones there please?"

Oh, yeah. And how.

"I am a fuckin' genius. I started everything," Jones spits out over the phone from his home in Los Angeles, laughing, this just beginning our half-hour of play, which people have not really heard the likes of since the Pistols split up 18 or so years ago.

Steve: "I'm a rebel."
Me: "Are ya?"
Steve: "No."
Me: "Sure you are."
Steve: "I am."

You know, the most fabulous thing about the Sex Pistols is you can chalk up every stupid thing they do or say to some kind of social experiment. Like Jones playing with Duran Duran's John Taylor (in the band Neurotic Outsiders, signed to Maverick) and living in Los Angeles. "What the…?" you start to say, before laughing knowingly. "Why that old rebel. Jeez. It's the ultimate punk thing to do. Playing with fuckin' John Taylor! Brilliant!"

We should all be so lucky to have such an easy way out of life's little embarrassments.

Anyway. Steve is on the line. Tell us about THEN, Steve. THEN. When punk was real and the streets was paved with hypodermic needles and people fuckin' pulverized each other pogo dancing, none of this fucking mosh-pit-safety-rules shite.

"It was out of control. It was fun sometimes. Sometimes it was miserable. But that was the way I was looking at things. Maybe it wasn't that bad. I was really glad it was over at the time. Then you have a few years to really, like, appreciate what we did for the universe, you know."

The universe, no less. Do tell.

"Well, we definitely opened the doors for people to be creative if they want to be and not be like stuck with certain rules that the record companies have for other people. We definitely changed the course of music whether you like it or I like it or not, you know."

OK. We've satisfactorily met the obligatory GIANT EGO portion of the ultimate rock interview.

Moving right along, we know John Lydon and Malcolm McLaren can talk a blue streak about how fuckin' postmodern it all was. What was your take on it, Steve? "Well, after a while, we definitely knew what was going on. That we was causing a lot of stir within society. Which is fantastic, because very rarely do you get that opportunity. It's tough being a legend."

Happy to take any credit coming his way (though he'd prefer cash) Jones still dismisses the notion that the Sex Pistols were part of some larger equation of personality, time and place that cannot be replicated now.

"Where I see it, the Sex Pistols are just a great fucking rock 'n' roll band. All the rest of it is just icing on the cake, really. I mean, no one ever saw us. There was no mystique about it. We never fuckin' played."

And so. Now, 20 years later, what can one expect? Are they better? Worse? Worse and therefore better? Better and therefore worse and therefore better?

No need to hurt yourself concocting your own theory when you have a live Sex Pistol happy to cut through everybody else's crap in order to drop a pile of his own.

"Well… we play the same three chords better."

MORE PISTOLS SHITE ON PAGE 22

PREVIEW
SEX PISTOLS
with Goldfinger, Gravity Kills
Monday, Aug. 12. Molson Amphitheatre.
$29.50/$35.50, 870-8000.

Steve Jones gives our lovely readers a salute while, inset, Paul Cook, Johnny Rotten, Glen Matlock and Jones prepare to count the money.

TOP 10 WORST THINGS PUNK HAS WROUGHT

1. The Goth movement (oh why, Siouxsie, why?!)
2. Sigue Sigue Sputnik's rehash of the EMI grab-and-dash cash scam
3. Ten or 15 more Ramones albums than were absolutely necessary
4. Anti-audience "punk" behavior from apparent non-punks like Billy Joel, Oasis and Bananarama
5. Platinum-selling bands from California who consider the second album by the Anti-Nowhere League as the pinnacle of achievement in 20th-century culture
6. The whole "not having to play your instruments" thing eventually causing nostalgia for Emerson, Lake And Palmer
7. The enduring mystique of Situationism
8. The use of the F-word in Alanis Morissette's "You Oughta Know"
9. Alt-rock critics' contempt for Frank Zappa
10. Kids paying money to go to a concert and then trying to kill each other using only their heads as weapons — **JASON ANDERSON**

TOP 10 POST-SEX PISTOLS CAREER HIGHLIGHTS

1. In 1984, "World Destruction" by Time Zone, a.k.a. Afrika Bambaataa and John Lydon, becomes the first and still only hip-hop/electro/punk/heavy metal single.
2. Steve Jones doesn't join The Power Station despite having every evident opportunity.
3. Late last year, Glen Matlock finally releases his autobiography, *I Was A Teenage Sex Pistol*, but still no one returns his phone calls.
4. Paul Cook doesn't play on Clash drummer Topper Headon's solo record, but does eventually join the band of avowed non-punk Edwyn Collins.
5. Founding member Keith Levene quits Public Image Ltd. when Lydon, distracted by a burgeoning film career in the mid-'80s, starts playing Sex Pistols songs again, something he swore he'd *never ever* do.
6. Steve Jones becomes the fourth-most reviled past-punk solo artist of the '80s after Billy Idol, Adam Ant and Peter Cetera.
7. Sid Vicious is portrayed in a movie by an actor who will go on to (much) less convincingly play Beethoven.
8. Approximately 183 Sex Pistols albums are released, with titles like *We Have Cum Far For Your Children*, *Chaos*, *Flogging A Dead Horse* and *The Swindle Continues*.
9. "Anarchy In The U.K." is covered by Megadeth, but they are compelled to Americanize the lyrics.
10. The *Filthy Lucre Live* CD is actually pretty good. — **J.A.**

Steve always stuck the fingers up in photos. I didn't smile in the pictures, because you can't smile and be cool.

John's tart card: a bit less graphic than the cards the rest of us had, but still an effective bit of design. He hadn't had his hair like that for years, though.

We rehearsed in Los Angeles beforehand for a month or so before the tour. I met up with John again and we chatted about business and did loads and loads of press. We'd booked a rehearsal place in the Valley, just over the Hollywood Hills. At first, John was quite cagey about getting up and singing with us. He had a six-pack of beer which he got through, but he still wouldn't get up and sing. Steve and Paul got fed up in the end and went home. I don't know if he was nervous or whatever, but I hung around a bit longer and there was a little bit of bonding between us, because I picked up Steve's guitar and then John got up and we went through the whole set. I thought, 'What's that all about?' It's funny, because there were a couple of Steve's fans listening outside, and I think they might have been a bit disappointed because they thought Steve's guitar playing wasn't up to scratch!

That place didn't work out because it was too hot, so we ended up rehearsing at this place that belonged to Guns N'Roses, because Steve was mates with them. Then Chris Thomas, our producer from the old days, came over and helped us routine the songs, although they didn't really need much routining. We were also gearing up to make a live record, so we had to relearn the songs: there was always a problem with John remembering the words.

We had a good crew. Bill, the production manager, sorted the gear out: Fender loaned me a bass. I've got a really nice old Bassman amp. It was very professional compared to the early days, although we always had good gear back in those days... thanks to Steve. We'd all been doing things to different degrees with different bands in the preceding years, so it didn't phase us. None of it did. We sorted out the songs by common consensus, just as we always did in the old days. Nobody really likes rehearsing, though: it's boring, but it's a necessary evil.

So, we had to remember the songs. I hadn't played them since 1977, and this was 1996, so you do the mathematics. It's hard to forget songs like 'Anarchy In The UK' and 'God Save The Queen', but for some of the other ones, you had to remember which bit came where. We had to get ourselves back up to match fitness, if you like: but then again, everyone had always been playing, so it wasn't like we had to relearn to play our instruments, we just had to relearn the songs. Steve and I tuned down a semitone, because John was singing a bit higher than he used to. We didn't tell him. Then again, I don't think anyone would know that unless you told them.

We didn't change the set much during the tour because we only had a certain number of songs to work with, although we did change the running

order from time to time. Paul seemed to like being in charge of that: he had a big whiteboard in the rehearsal room. John always had a big thing for 'Psychotic Reaction' but I don't think the rest of us have ever been that keen on it. It's the kind of song that doesn't really go anywhere: I think you have to be on acid to appreciate it.

In between rehearsing, we were at the Chateau Marmont hotel, doing press interview after press interview. One day, we were doing a photo session and we'd read in the paper that Kiss were reforming their classic line-up so we got all this makeup on.

Steve and I used to go out walking in the Hills when we were rehearsing. It's funny: you're rehearsing, but you don't rehearse that much. Little but often is the way. So you have a lot of time to fill, and Paul and I were in an apartment hotel, and you haven't got your things around you, so you want to get out and explore a bit.

I remember going mountain biking with Steve and Duff McKagan, who had just left Guns N'Roses. Steve was mates with Duff and introduced me to him: I thought he was a lovely bloke. I couldn't work the gears on my bike, though... that's my excuse and I'm sticking to it. They rode off into the distance and left me behind, with Steve laughing and saying I couldn't keep up because of all the cigarettes I smoke. They disappeared up Dead Man's Curve, which is a place up in Laurel Canyon or somewhere. I thought, 'Where did they go?' and when I looked where I thought they'd gone, I could just see them in the undergrowth in the distance. There was a track which was about 10 millimetres wider than the width of the tyres, and I made it down there, just about.

What I want to get across in this book is what it's like to be a married man with kids and go out and be a Sex Pistol. It's not always rock and roll all the time, because you're a bit older, but you see interesting things. You do amazing things, and you collect souvenirs, and you live well. You're not slumming it: we were designer punks; we always were, and we still are. This is what it's like behind the scenes. I want you to look at this and understand what a great thing it is.

In June, we headed for Europe for the first shows. As we went along I stuck everything in a box with the idea of doing a scrapbook one day, and here we are...

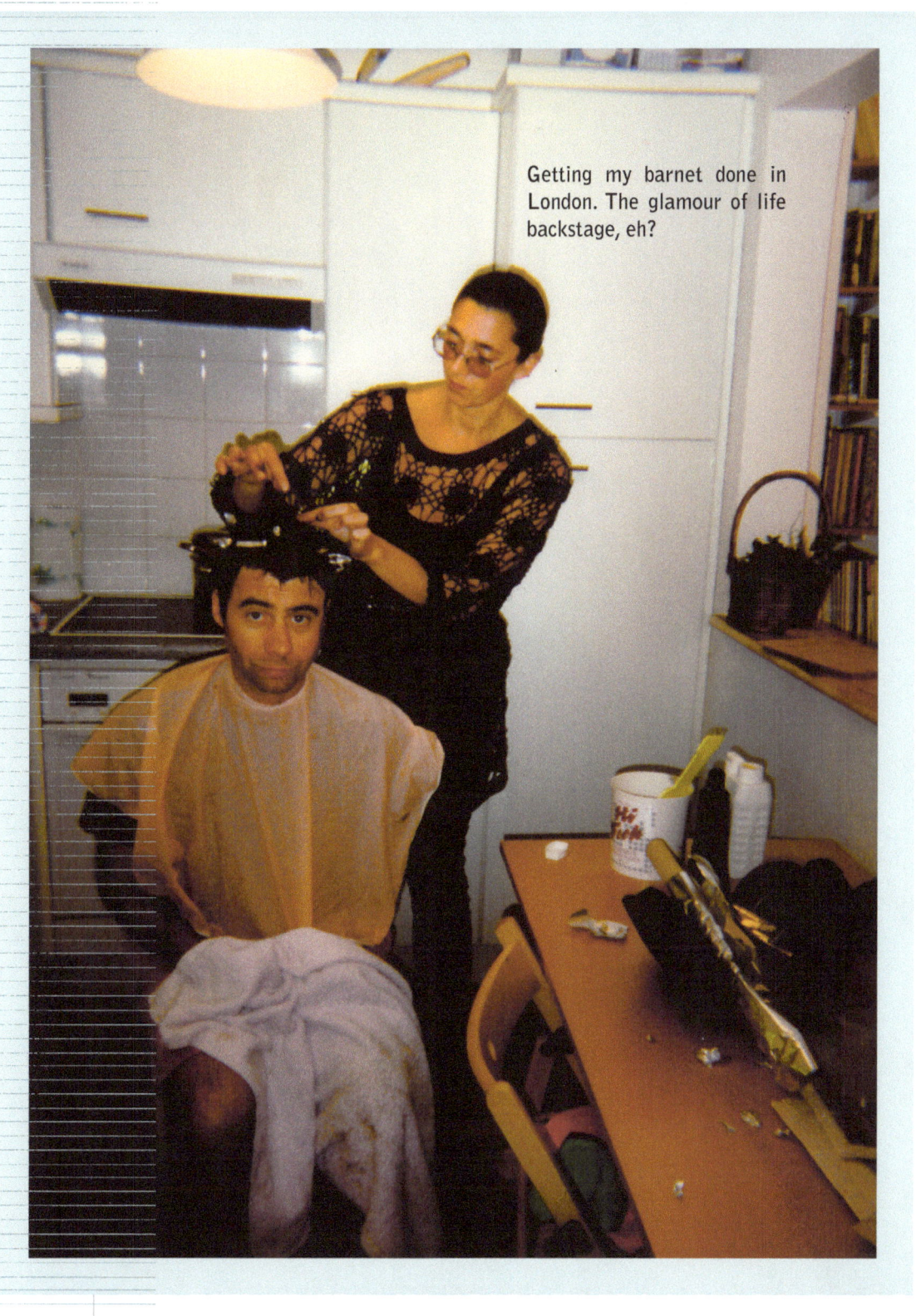

I'M COOKIE
I'LL BEAT MY MEAT

http://www.sexpistols.com
http://www.hob.com/sexpistols
Open 36 hours only

Paul's tart card, made up to look like he'd been stabbed by his own drumsticks. I always got on fine with Paul: he was a pleasure to play with. Sometimes when the vocals came in too early on stage, he and I would look at each other and communicate without speaking to get the song back on track.

BIZARRE
By Andy Coulson

PISTOL SHOTS

- THE Sex Pistols performed for the last time at San Francisco's Winterland Ballroom in January 1978. Rotten's last words to the crowd were: "Ever feel you've been cheated?" He left the band a week later.
- VICIOUS died of a heroin overdose on February 2, 1979 while awaiting trial for the murder of girlfriend Nancy Spungen.
- THE Pistols' most notorious performance was on Thames TV's Today show when they repeatedly swore, egged on by host Bill Grundy. He was later sacked.
- THE band never had a No 1. Their biggest hit was God Save The Queen which hit No 2 in 1977.
- ROTTEN has updated the famous image of the Queen with a safety pin through her face, using Diana's face instead.
- A LIVE album is planned but there will be no new material.
- THE band will play Finsbury Park, London, on June 23, SECC Glasgow, July 16, and Belfast Mayfield Leisure Centre, July 17.

Photos: DAVE HOGAN

PISTOLS RELOADED... from left, Cook, Lydon (Rotten), Jones and Matlock yesterday. Right, Lydon

NEVER MIND THE WRINKLES, HERE'S THE Sex Pistols

PUNK SHOCKERS... in '76, clockwise Matlock, rear left, Cook, Lydon, Jones

THE Sex Pistols launched their comeback yesterday with an hilarious Press conference.

John Lydon, Steve Jones, Glen Matlock and Paul Cook, all now 40, announced a world tour where they will thrash out punk favourites from their legendary 1977 album Never Mind The B*******s, Here's The Sex Pistols.

The shows, in Europe, the States and the Far East, are expected to net them around £750,000 each.

Their appearance together at the 100 Club in London's Oxford Street yesterday was their first since their split almost 20 years ago.

Matlock, the original bassist, had never forgiven the band after he was replaced by Sid Vicious, who died of a drug overdose in 1979.

There wasn't a safety pin in sight yesterday — instead the Pistols hid their middle-age spreads under trendy designer outfits. But like the old days it was Lydon — who will use his old name Johnny Rotten on tour — who talked most. Here are the best moments:

On their feud which barred previous reunions: "We don't see eye to eye but we have a common interest – your money.
"It is highly likely that we will just beat the c**p out of each other in the first three seconds of the show."

On Sid Vicious: "I was going to put a funeral urn on the table in his place today but unfortunately his ashes were blown all over Heathrow Airport some time ago. I would have needed a Hoover. But this is the original Pistols – Sid was nothing more than a coat hanger to fill an empty space on stage."

On the monarchy: "We are not trying to bring it down any more. Our very good fifth member, Lady Di, is doing an excellent job. We offered to do a benefit for her because she needs the cash."

On the money: "If you want to complain about people grabbing money, look at all the trashy little pop stars of today. Perhaps this is daylight robbery but who cares?"

On being seen as old farts: "I've enough old farts to spread over you lot if you don't shut your mouth.
"Like a fine wine I've matured with age. We love our beer bellies and you will too."

On plans for the Buzzcocks to support them: "Some geriatrics will perform before us but if you really want to enjoy yourself, come late."

On punks' habit of spitting at bands: "I never appreciated it. Spit this time and I'll retaliate more than in kind."

On playing Top Of The Pops: "We'll never perform on that show – it's so bad. But if they paid us, who knows?"

On rehearsals: "We won't bother. You know these songs as well as we do. I bet you play them better as well."

On their ageing fans: "I'm worried about the geriatrics that'll turn up. I hope it rains and they get their wheelchairs stuck in the mud."

Andy Coulson, writing about us in his Bizarre column. In 2011 he was arrested in connection with the ongoing phone-hacking scandal at the *News Of The World*, having resigned from his jobs twice — once as *NOTW* editor, once as David Cameron's Director Of Communications. Ah, the press...

21 June Messila Festival, Lahtis, Finland 22 June Roter Skeller Festival, Munich, Germany 23 June Finsbury Park, London, UK Sjohistoriska Museet, Stockholm, Sweden 25 June Roskilde Festival, Denmark 29 June Bahrenfield, Hamburg, Germany 30 June Open-Air Festival, St... Madrid, Spain (cancelled) 4 July Zeltpalast, Berlin, Germany 7 July Sportshalle, ... Tivoli, Ljubljana, Slovenia 10 July ... Parco Aquatica, Milan, Italy 13 July ... 14 July Unterfrankenhalle, Frankfurt... Scotland 17 July Maysfield Centre, Belfast, Northern Ireland (cancelled) 17 July Shepherd's Bush Empire, London, UK ... Ireland (cancelled) 20 July Axion Beach Festival, Zeebrugge, Belgium 21 July Phoenix Festival, Stratford-on-...

EUROPE

I'd become a bit cooler as a bass player in the interim: a bit less frantic. Certain things have a majesty and if you play them too fast, they lose something. On stage, performance adrenaline made all of us play a bit too fast at times, but Paul's always been good at timekeeping: if anything it was me and Steve who pushed the tempo a bit. Individually and collectively, we'd gained self-confidence and self-assuredness. No-one's style had changed dramatically, and anyway we wanted to sound like we did before, so we just played the same as we ever had. We were using Marshalls, so we sounded a bit bigger, but intrinsically the sound was the same. One of the best quotes I ever saw about Steve came from Nick Kent, who said, 'Steve had a lot of problems being knocked around by his stepfather, and his guitar sound was the sound of him paying his stepfather back.'

I had a spare bass which I blagged from Fender UK, a nice light Fender Precision sunburst. He told me I could have it on permanent loan. I wasn't sure if he meant I could have it, or if I had to ultimately give it back. We had this lighting guy who took a shine to this guitar, although I didn't actually use it: I used my white '61 Precision for most of the tour. On the very last gig of the tour, this guy, Jim, asked me to play this backup bass, and I asked why. He said he wanted it, and I said, 'I think I've got to give it back!' I played it anyway and then it was supposed to be shipped back to England… but it never made it back. The case was shipped back without it. I've never seen him since.

I'm a better bass player than a guitarist. I like playing bass when somebody else is singing, but when I'm singing and playing bass it's hard to put on so much of a show. You can be more of a showman when you're playing rhythm guitar. I'm getting pretty good at the bass, though. As a bass player, I play somewhere between the kick drum and the guitar riffs. I've always thought that Steve and Paul play well together and that the bass adds the tune. It's not the way most bass players look at it, but I've always dug bassists like James Jamerson. To me, *Never Mind The Bollocks* – although I'm not on most of it – is too black and white. I've always thought that the bass provides the colour and the counterpoint. Of course, you've got to be in tune and in time. I improvised a little on the bass this time: in the past I was sometimes guilty of playing too much, so I played less this time.

I started on an acoustic guitar, which is in the vault at the Hard Rock Café. I sold it years ago when I was skint: it paid the mortgage for several months. It's the guitar my mum and dad bought me when I was 10. Then I read somewhere that they had my guitar and I thought, 'That's funny, I don't remember selling that to them.' They've got Jimmy Page's Les Paul and all these other musicians' guitars – and mine. They showed me around and invited me to stay for the evening because they had a Nordoff-Robbins charity event with the characters from *The Fast Show*. It was fantastic. They asked me to get up and do the raffle, and while I was waiting to do that I saw Swiss Toni having a cigarette outside – it was really funny. Then Mark Williams, the guy who does the 'This week I have mostly been wearing…' routine, comes on stage. I'm sitting there with my son Louis, who was about 10 at the time, and he says 'Look! It's Ron Weasley's dad!' After the show Paul Whitehouse came up and said 'You must let me buy you a drink, I'm a huge fan of yours. You played the best gig of my life!' I said 'The Pistols?' and he said, 'No, you must get that all the time, I'd never say that to you. It was the Rich Kids in Cromer.' I said 'What on earth were you doing in Cromer?' and he told me that they all went to university in Norwich and they used to go down to Cromer. That was where they all met up'.

It's always surprising how many friends you've got when the Sex Pistols go on tour. People come out of the woodwork. Most of them are fine, though. They're not people who you don't want to put on the list; they're mostly people who just never get it together to go and buy a ticket. I'm guilty of that too, sometimes. It's just the way it is.

I put McGee on the guest list for Finsbury Park and he didn't come. I saw him a few days later and said, 'You didn't come!' and he went, 'Oh, I thought it would be a bit cabaret.' I said, 'Do you really think, Alan, that we would reform and go through all this just to be left with egg on our faces?' He said, 'I didn't think of it that way,' and later he came to the Shepherd's Bush Empire gig. We were supposed to be doing gigs in Ireland, which didn't happen for one reason or another – one was cancelled because they didn't sell enough tickets, and the other one was cancelled because they thought we'd be blasphemous, which I thought was a bit rich at the time given the sectarian violence there.

On that note, are we a political band? No. We were so apolitical that we were political. We never talked about it. It was never a sort of Politburo symposium like The Clash were. We said what was on our minds without recourse to the fact that you're probably not supposed to do that, but we didn't see that, which was construed as being political. I've never seen John occupying the City, and neither have I – although I did go down there once. I was with a mate who was having an eight-hour operation in hospital.

I went out to have a cigarette and walked around the corner and right into the back of the protest. Some guy comes up and says, 'Hey Glen, can you sing 'Anarchy In The UK' for us?' My mate was having this massive operation, so I said, 'Not at the moment, mate…' This guy got the hump. When you get recognised, you have to be on duty all the time, and people don't realise that you have other concerns.

Anyway, I suggested that we do a little club show instead of the Irish dates, and the agent came back with the Shepherd's Bush Empire, which was fantastic. So I told McGee he should come down, and he did, and he loved it. He asked the *NME* if he could write a review, but they wouldn't accept a review from him and said he could send it in as a letter. This wasn't good enough for him so he spent £12,000 to take out the back page as a review instead. It was an entire black page with white writing on.

My whole life had been in the shadow of the Sex Pistols, so the reunion turned things around for me, especially in terms of self-confidence. Finsbury Park proved us right. Some guy was having a go at John for the Sex Pistols selling out and playing stadiums like Finsbury Park, and John told him it wasn't a stadium, it was a field. When you do indoor shows the emotions are more contained. I like playing in tents, where you get the best of both worlds. But we had transcended venue size by this point. The gig I enjoyed playing most apart from Finsbury Park was the Shepherd's Bush Empire.

That gig meant a lot to us. When you're in a band, and it's going well, it's almost like it's what you've been put on earth to do. It feels right and it sounds right. You want to give a good account of yourself: that's my overriding standard. Whether this tour matched up to that aim is for other people to say, but we felt that we did a good job.

How did I feel when we stepped on stage for the first time together? I was excited, nervous, proud, concerned that we were going to make a mistake… all the emotions. It was completely different from the first time because nobody had been able to see us in the early days. People didn't know what to make of us at the time, but now it was a completely different thing. There was a huge sense of vindication – huge! It was an amazing experience to go through it all the first time and then come back.

The setlist stayed pretty much the same throughout the whole tour. It was put together by common consent. We'd say 'Well, that works,' or 'That doesn't work'. We might have swapped things around after the first few gigs, but once it was all working out, we stuck with it.

Funnily enough, the first two gigs of the tour weren't that great. We did some weird gig next to an ostrich farm in Finland, and everybody was a bit down about it, and then we did the second gig in Germany when it was pissing down with rain, and everybody was down after that one too.

But we kept going. That's an important point. We didn't cave in, and we never do.

But then we did Finsbury Park, the biggest show of the entire tour. We went on stage knowing that we were being recorded for the live album, and going out live on the radio at the same time – not a great idea! – and we also had to make a video, which was supposed to begin with us bursting through a fucking screen. All that, in front of 36,000 people.

What happened was, the night before I watched *Spinal Tap*, and there's a whole bit where the bass player gets caught in the pod – and the next day, we were in front of 36,000 people, going out live on the radio and recording a live album, recording a video and bursting through this paper, which was really thick cartridge paper. It had to be thick because the backdrop was massive: probably 60 feet by 40 feet in size. As I was about to burst throught it, all I could think of was the bass player being stuck in the pod, but luckily the roadies knew what was going on and they cut through the paper with a really fine slit so we could get through it. We only did it once: it must have cost a fortune.

It was funny, that gig: I was the first member of the band who got there. We had a portakabin in a field as a dressing room. Liam Gallagher was in there and I said 'Oi, you! Fuck off, you cheeky cunt'. I was kidding, though: he's a mate.

And then I bumped into Iggy Pop, who was also on the bill, and when he came off I was chatting to him. Iggy had it right, with his shirt off: he didn't have to worry about stage clothes. He was all sweaty with a towel wrapped around him and he said, 'Hi Glen, how are you guys doing?' He knew we were nervous. He deliberately didn't do 'No Fun' as well, just for us – although I think it was beneficial for him if we did the song and he didn't. That way it would be on the live album and he'd get some royalties.

It was a great gig, Finsbury Park.

NEVERMIND THE Sex Pistols

HERE COMES the FILTHY LUCRE TOUR

Guest list:- Terry Ward +1
Steve Klasson +1
Suzzanne Blomquist +1

TODAY IS :
Wed, Jun 26, 1996

COUNTRY : Sweden
TEL. CODE : 46

	BAND PARTY	CREW PARTY
PRE SHOW TRAVEL :	Vans to s'check at 1.30 approx. then return to hotel. Dep. for gig at 6.30 approx.	Vans to s'check...probably stay at gig until a'show.

VENUE : Sjohistoriska Museet Garden
(Naval History Museum Garden)
Djurgardsbrunnsvagen,
Stockholm, Sweden

CAPACITY : 10000
DOORS: 4:00 PM
SEX P: 8:30 PM
TEL :
FAX :

Record show?

PROMOTER Thomas Johansson
EMA Telstar
Box 18, 18121 Lidingo,
Stockholm, Sweden

BAND HOTEL : Radisson SAS Strand
Nybrokajen 9
P.O. Box 16396
Stockholm, Sweden S-103 27

CREW HOTEL As band.

TEL:
FAX:

AFTER SHOW TRAVEL BAND : Stay in Stockholm.

AFTER SHOW TRAVEL CREW : As band.

Jean Michel Cohard +1
Marc Zermatti +1
Freddie Lynn +1
Carol Barres +1
Michel Vidal +3
Gissette Hosburg +1
Pascal +1

TODAY IS :
Thu, Jul 4, 1996

COUNTRY : France
TEL. CODE : 33

BAND PARTY	CREW PARTY
Checkout and bus to s'check.	Checkout and bus to load in.

PRE SHOW TRAVEL :

VENUE : Zenith
211 Ave. Jean Jaures,
75019 Paris
(B'stage entrance is via B'lvrd Mc. Donald).

CAPACITY : 6000
DOORS: 6:45 PM
SEX P: 9:15 PM
TEL :
FAX :

PROMOTER Alain Lahana
Canal Productions
20 Ave. de la Villette
75019 Paris

BAND HOTEL : Relais Carre D'Or,
46 Avenue George V,
Paris, France 75008
(Until 4pm only).

CREW HOTEL   None.

TEL:
FAX:

AFTER SHOW TRAVEL BAND :
Bus overnight to Berlin - 680 miles plus border, approx. 14hrs.

AFTER SHOW TRAVEL CREW :
As band.

HOW WERE THEY FOR YOU?
② THE SEVENTIES

When the *Melody Maker* asked me what I'd thought of the Seventies as a decade, I didn't want to play their nostalgia game. I thought the music scene in the Nineties was just as healthy as it had ever been back then. Opportunities for kids to play music and form bands were more common now than ever before, even if some critics regarded the Seventies as some kind of golden age.

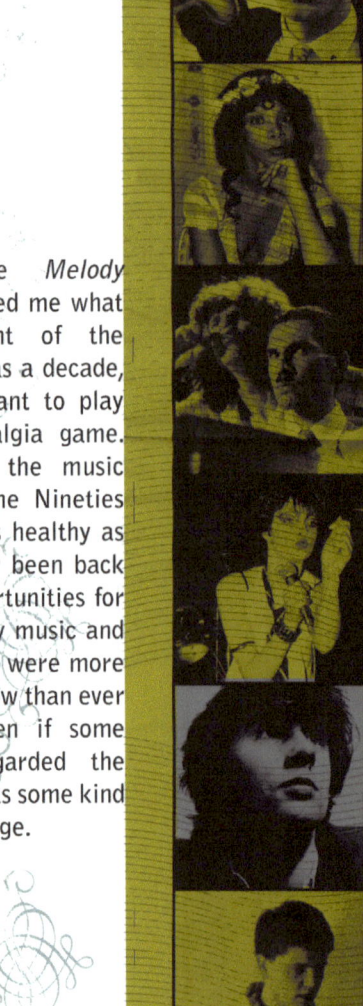

EDWYN COLLINS, BRITPOP PIONEER

"AFTER you got past the Bamo thing that some silly people at Melody Maker are trying to revive, the Eighties seemed like a period of good taste – the designer decade. The Seventies seemed really kitsch, and still does to some extent.

"The turn of the decade coincided with me going to secondary school and taking pop music more seriously. Initially it was the glam-rockers like Roxy Music, Sparks, Bowie and Lou Reed. My Mum liked the glam-rockers, but my Dad was totally taken aback when Bowie came out in Melody Maker in '72, saying, 'Hi, I'm bi!' That was really outrageous at the time.

"In Glasgow in '76/'77, everybody was wearing baggy trousers like The Stone Roses! Older people wore conservative flares, and the youth wore 'baggies' that flared out from the waist. I first wore straight trousers in '76. Where I lived, that was reason enough for people to want to beat you up!

"There was far more aggro and religious bigotry. In Glasgow, there were pitched battles in the streets on Saturday between Celtic and Rangers fans, especially around the 'Old Firm' matches. It's calmed down a bit now.

"There wasn't really the diversity of music that there is now. There were just people who were into soul, people who were into glam and people who were very proud of being into 'progressive'. Progressive and metal crossed over. The same people who had the King Crimson and ELO albums also had 'Black Sabbath Vol 4', which was the 'Nevermind' of its day. 'Paranoid' was the 'Smells Like Teen Spirit', and the Blur versus Oasis of then was T Rex versus Slade!

"I'm sure there are Seventies references in my music. I don't want to re-sell my youth to a new generation, but I don't despise my youth, and I don't have any regrets."

DONNA SUMMER, DISCO DIVA

"I WAS in Germany, and what hit Britain and the States in the Sixties snowballed into Europe later. I was in the musical 'Hair' in 1970, and that was from the era of dope-smoking! I'd travel back and forth from Germany to England, and there were always friends I could stay with. If I had money and they needed it I'd give it to them; if I needed money, the same thing. The youth got more active in politics, and people were letting go of a lot of rules and regulations.

"It wasn't until the late Seventies when the drugs started to get out of hand. We lost a lot of great musicians: Janis Joplin, Jim Morrison, Jimi Hendrix. Those were the first signs that we'd better be careful, when someone famous made a mistake. That was the worst thing.

"Although I think a lot of people would say that it was the clothes I still like them! All right, certainly not all of the polyester, but I loved bell-bottomed pants! I'd still wear 'em now. I'm not ashamed of anything I wore at the time – it was fun, it was away from the norm!

"One of the few things that really surprises me in this generation is tongue rings! How do you talk, how do you swallow? At least nothing we did was painful! If it didn't feel good, we didn't do it!

"People will always want to dance, so dance music, whether you call it disco, hip hop, house or rave, will mutate and keep going. I still like a lot of songs I hear. To me, alternative rock now is very much Seventies music. It's very much, 'Listen to what I have to say.'"

RON MAEL, SPARKS

"WE moved to England in '73 and got lots of attention, much to our amazement. I remember that after we had recorded our album ['Kimono My House'] there was an energy crisis, and we were told that there might not be any vinyl to press our album! Fortunately, that turned out to be a little exaggerated.

"We would come back to the Whiskey-A-Go-Go in Los Angeles and they would put on the billboard 'From Britain'! We thought it was pretty humorous – and also flattering. We always thought that American music was less exciting than a lot of what was going on in Europe.

"I tried to look old in the Seventies. I'm only embarrassed in that some of the irony of that attempt has worn off today!

"One thing I really feel strongly about is that it seems like music with any kind of charm is seen as having a kind of preciousness about it, that it's too quaint. I think that's the major difference between music now and the better music of that period. One strength of British music now is that at least a certain amount of that is accepted, where in America there's none of that.

"It's a generalisation, but I think that maybe music matters less to people now, because there are so many other things that you can do, and any time that there's a movement that's against the standard, it gets sucked up by the television.

"It seems that immediately, your song is being used for a beer commercial, so it's difficult to have that stance of being a rebel. Even if it wasn't truly the case in the Seventies, at least there was some of the appearance of that."

SIOUXSIE SIOUX, POST-PUNK QUEEN

"IT'S very difficult to think of the Seventies as one thing. The Seventies was a real mix of styles. The beginning was the left-overs from the Sixties, and bands like Pink Floyd having a firm foothold. Then you had this transition with people like T Rex, Roxy Music and Bowie, and then you had punk rock at the end.

"The best thing was threatening some people who thought they had very secure jobs in the music industry. It put a firecracker up the music industry. The irony is that the worst thing is some of the people who are still around now. There's even a Rutles revival, so what has changed?

"I think a loss of naivety is the big difference now. It has all become big business. And I think that the independent labels and MTV coming along would have opened things up a lot more, but I think it's closed things down and narrowed the vision. Being in America, when you've got 60 channels to choose from, and you actually haven't. They show you what they want you to see.

"Artists like Tom Waits, for instance, how often do you see him on MTV? And he's made some great videos, and been very influential.

"My three favourite albums from last year were Tricky, Radiohead and Garbage. There are good things going on, but I certainly don't think that the media's reporting on things should be seen as the Bible.

"I really can't understand this sudden nationalistic thing that's going on. It's self-perpetuating and self-congratulatory, and I wouldn't want to be a part of it. I certainly don't believe that all that's British is bloody wonderful."

GLEN MATLOCK, SEX PISTOL

"FLARES, denims, blues bands, pub rock, punk rock, glam... it was a real mish-mash.

"The best thing for me, I suppose, was reading the papers on the morning after the Bill Grundy show. That just felt like we'd arrived and we'd got our foot in the door. What door to where, though, I'm not sure!

"The worst single thing was the time I had to share a launderette bag with my mate at the Reading Festival in '73! We didn't have a tent, so we dossed down in this launderette bag right in front of the gates so we could be first in. We were about a mile further back when we woke up. I think someone must have bodily lifted us up and dumped us!

"I think music is worse now. I think there was a lot more innovation then, and you could shake up things on a more regular basis. But then, things are a lot healthier now, in the middle of the Nineties, than they have been for a long time. Oasis have gone for America head-on, and they're reaping the benefits of that.

"It must be great for kids now because they've got such a wealth of things to draw on, but on the other hand maybe that gets a bit confusing. I think things are a lot straighter these days, a lot more corporate. People are less willing to take risks. I think that's a direct result of Thatcher's Britain, when people kept their heads down because they were afraid of losing their jobs.

"It's kind of weird that the '1999' record [by 4] was written in 1980. Perhaps someone should write a new one. Maybe I'll do it!"

ALAN HORNE, HEAD OF POSTCARD RECORDS

"I NEVER saw punk as doing away with the hippies. What *did* do away with the hippies was the Eighties, and all that desperate capitalism. Punk was an art movement that probably would have been admired by the hippies if it had been dressed up differently.

"The Seventies was a dreadful time for me, but in hindsight it seems fantastic because things got much, much worse afterwards. All the things I care about in life got really f***ed up. I suppose the Seventies was the last time when interesting, smart, motivated and inspired people were working in the arts.

"I wouldn't tell you that punk was good musically. It was rubbish. Glam was good musically. Marc Bolan's stuff still stands up to this day. There was a lot of innovation in the Seventies and there's been none in the Nineties, it's just all down to whatever sampled sound you can dig up. Lyrically, nobody's saying anything new.

"There was still a sense of optimism in the Seventies, as it was still possible to do things on a smaller scale and confound people's expectations. There were intelligent people in the media, too, whereas now it's all people from my generation making careers for themselves, so you get rubbish like the Tony Parsons' TV show.

"Then there was that whole punk nastiness – hating everything. The Seventies really taught young people to be cynical. A lot of people choose to put on this horrible American fake happiness; this well-adjusted thing: 'Hey, everything's fine'. That's just not me, and I don't see any point in faking it.

"I suppose that's why I'm such a nasty, cantankerous old git!"

INTERVIEWS: DAVE JENNINGS

I had no problem with Sid Vicious. He was a likeable nitwit, although he had problems. I put my foot down and said I wasn't having pictures of him on the backdrop for the live shows, though. In the end we used the beercan shot, which is pretty iconic: it's even in the National Portrait Gallery.

John had described Sid as a 'coathanger' at the press conference in London, meaning that Sid looked good in a leather jacket, which he did. Sometimes I think John was hard on Sid for my benefit, because all he did in the band was steal the limelight. I've said this before: when I was in the band I was happy to be the bass player and let John be at the front, but Sid craved so much attention that it upset the balance. I was the opposite: I didn't say anything on stage because I don't think you should. I think you should let the frontman be the frontman. I've got plenty of things to say, but I say them when I'm the frontman in my band. Also, if you speak into the backing vocals microphone, it's usually not loud enough, so no-one can hear you and you look like an idiot. I found that out from experience.

In this interview I said that music was healthier in 1996 than it had been in the '70s because guitar-based music was starting to come back. It's the same in 2013, except nobody sells any records any more.

Some writers criticised us for supposedly lacking 'danger'. Why would anyone think there was there was going to be any danger in a band that had come from 1976 and '77? This was all about social context. You can't divorce the original Pistols from the historical place and time where we were. This time round, we were playing our own music, a fact that was completely ignored the first time around, even by our manager. It was only a few years before this that Malcolm realised that we were any fucking good.

LACKING DANGER

They're back! They're very rude! And they want a fight! They are, of course, the **Sex Pistols**. So, as the four angry old men prepare for their comeback gig in front of 30,000 at Finsbury Park, a bitter, egotistical (it says here) GAVIN MARTIN puts it to them straight — do they just want your filthy lucre or do they mean it, maaan? Pistol shots: KEVIN CUMMINS

'I WANT YOU ALL TO LICK MY

Mr John Lydon is drowning in a sea of sake and a lake of lager. Johnny Rotten — Sex Pistol, relentless antagonist and caustic clown — is taking over.

At times during the meal in this Japanese restaurant, not far from Lydon's Los Angeles home or the Marina Del Ray Motel where the Sex Pistols have been doing interviews all day, he seemed to be in reasonably amiable form. Despite his habit of belching and expectorating loudly and persistently while we ate, despite extending his talent for instant mimicry to the Oriental waitress, he'd often guffaw merrily between stories and pronouncements.

When he claimed PiL had inspired some great groups, the photographer reminded him he'd opened the door for a lot that were awful too. Not for the first time he nodded and laughed, proffering his hands across a table littered with sake jugs, slapped palms and yelled. "Arrrrrbaaa"; his favourite new war cry.

Paul Cook and Steve Jones, perhaps wise to the ways of he who is Rotten, had bowed out after the interview. But his chauffeur for the evening, a sober Glen Matlock Esquire, is sat at the other end of the table. They seem to be getting along. Earlier in the motel, when Matlock asked for room service, Rotten was his usual haughty self.

"If you want room service, I want rim service…. I want you all to lick my arse."

"But we do that anyway John, all the time," grinned Glen, learning to live with the monstrous Rotten ego all over again.

Now they talk about the old days, exchange and demand outrageous rumours about current pop stars and recall the "genius" Steve Jones displayed for stealing and wheeler-dealing when the Sex Pistols were struggling to get started.

> "When you went down to the public lavs in Piccadilly Circus they'd say, 'You're one of them Sex Pistols. Prove it.'" — Steve Jones

Matlock: "We didn't have ten quid between us and he'd con his way into a sponsorship deal for guitar strings or amplifiers."

Rotten: "This time we hope to get him to play a few guitars, not just steal them."

After slurping up a plate of monkfish liver in soy sauce, Hannibal Lecter-style, one of his few recourses to 'solids' during the evening, Rotten roars through a football terrace chant version of 'Pretty Vacant', talks about music he likes — Black Grape, Suede, Jamaican reggae — friends, family and Ireland, land of his forefathers and, ironically, the place where he suffered the most intensified post-Pistols backlash of them all — regularly beaten up while held, on subsequently dismissed charges, in a Dublin jail in 1979. He has never been back.

Then suddenly the alcohol-lubricated switch in his brain goes PING! and Johnny remembers — he does not want to be a gracious dinner guest, he does not want to be friendly. Johnny Rotten is flying high, spoiling for a fight and he is seated opposite a representative from the 'evil empire' that is NME.

Remember his first historic single, 'Anarchy In The UK', and its brazen call to arms — "I use the NME, I use anorchee"? And its equally coruscating B-side, 'I Wanna Be Me' — a howling nightmare of media paranoia — "You wanna ruin us in your magazine/You wanna cover us in margarine"? The battle lines were drawn years ago.

Now he fixes me with a stare and asks me to hit him. "I do not like you. You are a c—," he says in

Never mind the dog's bollocks… a charming sight, eh readers?

that whining dentist-drill voice. Perhaps I look like I've come to cover him in a popular butter substitute. He rains down a hailstorm of hatred and bitter enmities, decides I'm a closet queen scared to come out, casts up a vision of his friends in London and what they'll do should I incur their displeasure. Or his. He dares me to move and he'll strike a blow. For liberty. For the Sex Pistols. For the hell of it.

"Go on try it. You think I wouldn't?"

Everything freezes, the table goes silent. How weird — a playground face-off with a middle-aged man.

Is Johnny serious? Or is this just the comeback kid in training, psyching himself up for a showdown with his own history. Throughout the course of the day, rearing between the lines of Lydon's posturing, sarcasm and antics, it's not hard to see Lydon/Rotten as a desperate man, besieged, fighting to reclaim his heritage. Who can blame him? In the short time they were together, the Sex Pistols, the original Sex Pistols before they were joined by the late, and, junkie clown Sid Vicious, laid out a legacy as potent and lasting and endlessly inspiring as any in rock'n'roll history. Kurt Cobain, Liam Gallagher, Shaun Ryder and hundreds more were powered to life, driven to new heights by the Pistols, a veritable howling cultural hurricane.

Pundits and academics have analysed and deconstructed their continuing potency, former manager Malcolm McLaren burned his effigy at the stake in The Great Rock'n'Roll Swindle. Now Johnny Rotten, the guy at the centre of the storm, wants his due, wants his filthy lucre and his respect. Johnny Rotten — Lydon's alter ego — is a lazy sod with a heart of fire, Stig Of The Dump mutating into a flabby white ghost. But Johnny Rotten is the force that set him free from the penury and the stasis of his life in north London 20 years ago. Past connections are important to Lydon, they were important to him when he recorded 'Open Up' with Leftfield, this decade's most potent blast of Rotten roll. But when the duo, friends for 15 years, asked him to join them on the road, he smirked at the idea.

Johnny Rotten as celebrity sideshow, the caterwauling demon king pushed into a cameo role? Noooo. Not yet, anyway. Johnny is shaping up for a fight for his life, or at least a significant part of it. In what could be the most extraordinary or the saddest world tour in rock'n'roll history.

Now we sit eyeball-to-eyeball, until the tension breaks, until the switch goes PING! again. Until Johnny shakes his head and announces, "I don't care, I really don't care about any of it any more."

The Sex Pistols 1996. Come and have a go if you think you're hard, or drunk, enough…

BUT WATCH out for Winston. Early in the afternoon, Steve Jones is sprawled on a double bed in a beach-front motel room kissing Winston, his fully-grown boxer dog, full on his big, wet lips. But Johnny, stoking his thirst with the first of God knows how many beers, does the barking.

"Yes, we know Gavin, his ego and reputation goes before him," he sneers. He sizes me up. "I know what you're about, you're a very bitter man. I've read your articles."

Ego. Reputation. Bitter mankier? Takes one to know one, that's what they say, isn't it, sir?

Rotten is a fiery eyeball of antipathy. Jones is a canned tattooed LA d London wide boy, a reformed junkie/alcoholic/kleptomaniac who now attends AA meetings but remains an unredeemed vulgarist. But what about Winston, is he trained?

"Yeah, you want him to bite you? Nah, he's not like that — he's a love dog. I've trained him to suck willies."

Really.

Rotten: "Wanna see his teeth, mmm, it's delicious. It's the dog that united us, once he taught it to give blow jobs that was it. Poor old slobby."

Oral bestiality and animal transvestism aside (later Jones reveals the dog "looks great in high heels"), how will the Pistols cope with playing to 30,000 at Finsbury Park? After all, they played their biggest gig to an audience of 5,000 in San Francisco in January 1978 and promptly split. And that was long after Matlock was sacked.

Jones: "Doesn't really matter whether it's the 100 Club or whatev. We'll just play 'Never Mind The Bollocks and B-sides. Some cover versions, 'Stepping Stone', stuff like that. I'm sure everyone's going to have it but who cares."

Rotten: "Hello, look this is the Sex Pistols. We've never laid an audience that appreciated or understood or even liked us from when we originally existed, so what's the f—ing difference? It's the same animosity, it's the same bullshit, it's just dressed in different f—ing artillery. Oooh yer old, yer fat, yer this…, whatever, it doesn't matter. It's the same nonsense.

"Odd nobody has accused us of not being able to play. Actually no, the slyness is because you're 40 years old you can't play. It's the same weapon, it's just disguised."

Some people are quite excited about the idea of seeing the Sex Pistols.

"They probably are but none of them are journalists."

I am.

"No you're not, I know what you're about. I know who you write for. It is the industry you write for, the industry doesn't like bands this through the industry. The industry uses Kiss. Nobody slags that reunion, but us — it's something else. This shouldn't happen, good things should be left alone. What good things?

"Nobody ever said a f—ing good word to us in our entire life about anything. Ever. We've never got idiot things like respect."

Loads of groups pay homage to the Pistols.

"Bands, general public, but not the press. This is

"Nobody ever said a f—ing good word to us in our entire life about anything. Ever. We've never got idiot things like respect." — Johnny Rotten

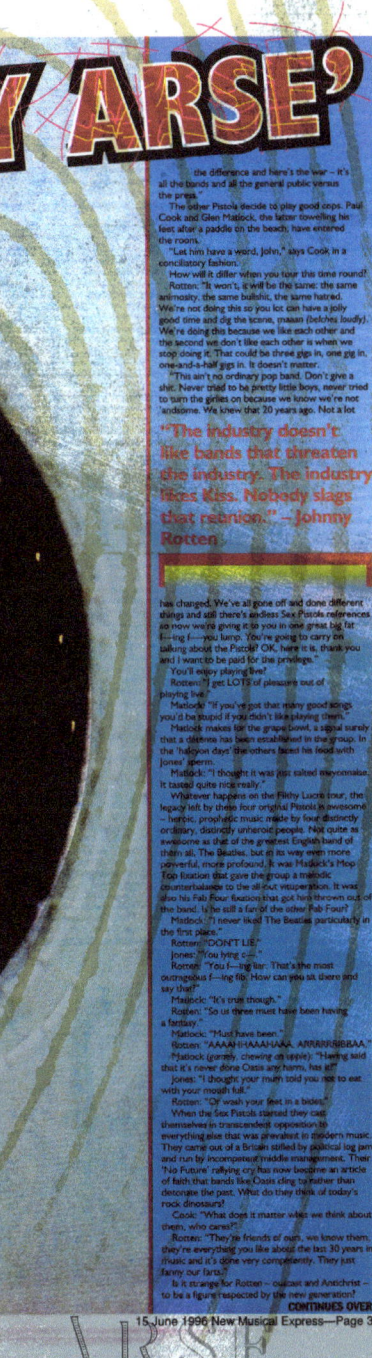

Not much anarchy in the UK today

Caitlin Moran *finds little left of the punk revolution after joining fans on the way to the Sex Pistols' reunion in north London*

THE road to London's Finsbury Park, where the Sex Pistols yesterday staged their much-hyped reunion, is littered with the debris of the punk revolution, 1996 style.

Three or four dozen men in their late thirties, wearing faded Sex Pistol T-shirts, were slumped in semi-conscious, beery heaps. The revolution will be something they read about in the newspapers and see on television.

The teenagers who had turned out seemed to feel they had missed out on the youth ferment of the 1960s and 1970s. "Oasis and Blur are rubbish," Nathan, 18, said. "They are not anything to get excited about. Most British music is boring".

"We are here to see Iggy Pop and the Pistols — but it's been quite dull so far." James, 17, said. "I thought there would be a bit of excitement; someone might wreck the ice-cream vans or the burger stalls."

And indeed, if the audience were expecting a second attempt at the punk revolution, which produced such notorious Pistols' numbers as *Anarchy in the UK*, they were disappointed.

But when punk emerged in the 70s it was somewhat bungled — tours were cancelled, inter-band squabbling diluted any clear punk ethos, and most of the prime movers happily took their profits when it fizzled out. The real changes that punk brought about were within the music industry: the Pistol's Finsbury support band, the Buzzcocks, started a trend for independent, band-managed labels.

Any feelings that today's youth may have about "missing out" can be put down to self-celebratory PR by retired punks and hippies. However, judging from the Pistols' rather muted reunion last night, there is nothing to be nostalgic about: save for the fact that attending such a gig in the 1970s would have cost £1; rather than £25, plus parking, plus T-shirt, plus programme, plus babysitter . . .

Lick my arse – that was a great comment, made by John at the press conference. They knew what he was saying and it was all part of the game they wanted to play. As for Caitlin Moran's review of Finsbury Park in *The Times*, when she basically said it was boring, well bless her, I say. The fact that she thought it was boring says a lot more about her than it does about the Sex Pistols.

FUCKOFFYO

56

The *NME*. I have never in my life attempted to look hard: I just do what I do. That bloke has no idea of what was going through my mind. He's a wanker. He probably thought that Menswear were going to be number one all over the world.

We did *Top Of The Pops* on June 28, 1996. We played 'Pretty Vacant' and 'New York'. Joe Strummer was there at the same filming. Joe saw John afterwards and said to me, 'Maybe I should go and say hello?', so I said 'Go on then,' and he said, 'I don't know if I should,' so I said, 'Well don't then!' Then he did, but John tore a strip off him and he came back with his tail between his legs.

A word about how I wrote 'Pretty Vacant'. At the time, there was a lot of talk from music writers about movements such as nihilism and Dadaism, and some of the stories about us in the music press stressed those elements of what we did pretty heavily. I'd learned about these things from my reading list for the modern art section of my art college foundation course, and when I wrote songs at the time what I was trying to do was keep the focus on simplicity. I wanted to use good ideas, but strip them right down to their most essential parts. From the beginning, the important thing was to get across the concept behind the band in the songs of the band. Essentially, our job was to turn meaning into sound.

I wrote the lyrics to 'Pretty Vacant', apart from a couple of lines in the second verse that John changed later on. My original lines were along the lines of 'If you don't like this, up yer bum, we're going down the pub'. John changed it to 'Forget your cheap comments, we know we're for real', which is obviously a far better lyric, but the core of the song is mine.

I couldn't quite get the tune right though: I needed a particular musical idea which would echo the lyrical idea. Eventually an idea came to me in Moonie's, which was an upstairs bar in Charing Cross Road, across the street from the Cambridge Theatre. I was in there one lunchtime, drinking my way through my dole money when Abba's 'SOS' came on the jukebox. I heard the riff on it, one simple repeated pattern. I took that pattern and altered it slightly, adding the fifth between the root note and the octave. It couldn't be simpler.

After that, I fitted the chord sequence to the chorus. That came straight from the Small Faces' 'Wham Bam, Thank You Ma'am', just because it was a great fit.

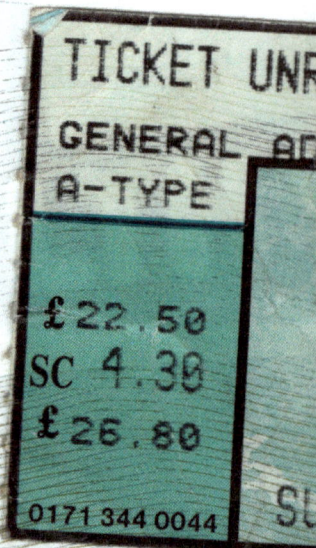

'Pretty Vacant' is a simple song, which was deliberate. If you're going to be simple, you should be as simple as you possibly can. 'Boredom' by the Buzzcocks is a perfect example of this. The one-note guitar solo expresses exactly what the song is about. That simple riff is the very centre of 'Pretty Vacant'. It establishes the basic idea and feeling of the song. We could have sat around playing complex chords: believe me, if we'd applied ourselves in that direction, we would have been quite capable of doing it. Instead, we deliberately chose to go our own way, keeping it as basic as possible.

Funny how no-one noticed that 'Pretty Vacant' is nicked from 'SOS' until I wrote *I Was A Teenage Sex Pistol* all those years later. But that's what songwriting is all about. Everything is nicked from something else. Only years after you've written the song do you let on.

I remember a similar thing happened years ago when I was touring with Iggy Pop. We were in a hotel in Detroit or somewhere, and James Brown came into the lobby with his entourage and stood about six feet from where we were sitting. Iggy said to me, 'He's my hero! I should say hello, but I can't.' I said, 'You might never see him again, go and say hello' so he went up to him, tapped him on the shoulder and said 'Hello Mr. Brown, my name is Iggy Pop and I'm a singer too.' James Brown turned around and said, 'So what?' and walked off. Iggy came back and sat down, looking at me as if it was my fault. I said, 'Hey, at least you met him!'

At the Roskilde festival in Denmark, we got bottled off. There was a fucking hail of them, so we stopped and went off, and then came back on again, but a beer can missed Paul's head by an inch, so we went off again. The promoter spoke to them, but the bottles kept coming. In the end the promoter said to us, 'Don't go back on. I'll still pay you, but it's just too dangerous for you to play.' It was the biggest gig I've ever done – 125,000 people – and it was ruined by a few idiots in the front row, who we think were members of one of the other bands on the bill. At one point a big champagne bottle just missed me: it would have hit me if I hadn't pulled back a bit just in time. You could lose an eye. There was supposed to be no glass at the gig: the only glass in the place was from the hospitality, which is why we think it was something to do with one of the other bands.

There was a problem with the PA in Paris, though – not a major problem that affected the sound for the people in the crowd, but the PA was cutting out intermittently and they couldn't use any of it in the mobile studio. When we were choosing the material for the album, we could either pick the best songs from all three shows or just use the best gig, so we ended up using the Finsbury Park show.

I thought the album didn't sound as good as the BBC's live broadcast. I don't know why: it just didn't, even though it was exactly the same gig. I remember the Brixton show was the same, I went and listened to it and I told Chris that the bass sounded hollow and too far back. He fiddled around with it: in 5.1 you can move where the centre of the stereo is in three dimensions, which is useful.

BOTTLES KEPT

Jun 28, 1996

Passenger vans from ... to gig at 10 ...

Roskilde Festival- Orange ...
Dyrskuepladsen - Gate ...
4000 Roskilde, Denmark

Contact:

COMING

Albums

A review of the live album and the *Never Mind The Bollocks...* reissue. One thing I've found in my life is that it's very easy to be cynical. It's the path of least resistance.

SEX PISTOLS
NEVER MIND THE BOLLOCKS/SPUNK
Virgin
(33 tks/108 mins)
FILTHY LUCRE – LIVE
Virgin
(15 tks/53 mins)

COLT IN THE ACT

First, the reissue of the one 'great' album, complete with demos, then the arrival of a live record of Finsbury Park. How much do you need to hear of THE SEX PISTOLS?

AND so they're slotted in, the punk chapter in every Big Book Of Rock, flick through the index and they'll be there between Santana and Del Shannon in bold type; the next time they do one of those 100 Best Albums Of All Time radio votes they'll be nestling neatly at about number twenty-six, betwixt Blonde On Blonde and Dark Side Of The Moon, processed, placed, understood. McLaren, born smirking and uncaring, will recline with a cigar and a smug sense of vindication and wait for his cheques. The band will stand another round in the local. Lydon, who you hope is past caring, will fly home and feed his plants and die. The Sex Pistols are history, meaningful figures, boring, everything they resisted, everything it was inevitable they'd become. But "Never Mind The Bollocks, as a human transmission, as a piece of plastic, as an idea, even through the putrid rose-tints of retrospect, even with the distance of time and the accumulation of official sanction, is still a bomb beyond appraisal, impossible, UNDENIABLE.

I was five when this was released. It sparks no recollections. I remember Sham 69 on "Tiswas", The Boomtown Rats, Sid Snot, "Vague", and that's punk for me. But "Bollocks" reaches over time, culture, memory and f***ing chokes you. "Holidays In The Sun" engulfs you, with too many thoughts, too much to be sated, a sound that's still unsurpassed, still unmediable, still resistant to everything but its own demented logic. "Bodies" is the closest music has ever got to pure nihilism, grooves steeped and knee-deep in loathing, gasping in disgust, sinking in infinite hatred. "Anarchy" will place demands on the rest of your life if you are mad enough to let it, "Pretty Vacant" is for jukeboxes and Dave Lee Travis, the rest is kindling or gospel depending on your mood or your inclination.

What's true is that it's all uncomfortable, all unbreakable, it's all still here, out of time, but creating its own context in '96 as you let it in. What's curious is how a band of chancers and ne'er-do-wells could pretty much perfect rock music 30 years after it started and 20 years before it began to die. No other band before or since had sounded quite so driven, quite so urgent, quite so up at you and gouging. What's weird is that Johnny Rotten's voice doesn't sound like a relic from a bygone age, it sounds as unanswerable and distressingly human as it ever did. What's strange is that this stuff touches you, after 20 years that have been cursed by its continued worship and acceptance.

Oh, forget the live LP (not because it's sad or a betrayal or a live album, just because it's dull, basically, "Bollocks" with a sagging paunch and a few thousand cider-punk screams) and forget the extra tracks (on "Spunk", the bootleg demo LP hawked about before the original release of "Bollocks"; interesting for the deeper wail of Lydon's proto-P.i.L. vocals but not much else). Forget the filling in of gaps in the story (stories have endings), the footnotes and footholds and explanations. Forget the archaeology and listen to "Holidays In The Sun". It makes you want to change the world, it makes you want to kill the Pistol's stranglehold on pop for good and go one better. That's all that matters, that's enough for now.

NEIL KULKARNI

Sex Pistols
Filthy Lucre Live

The *Filthy Lucre Live* album came out on July 29, only a month or so after the Finsbury Park show. Chris Thomas came out to record three gigs: one in Germany, which wasn't a great gig, I don't know why, then Finsbury Park and then the one in Paris.

SEX PISTOLS

"I changed my mind. That does not make me a [bleeping] hypocrite, you [bleeping bleep bleep bleep]."

— Johnny Rotten

The tour went well, with very few cancelled dates. One of the shows in Ireland was pulled because they thought it was going to be blasphemous, which I thought was cheeky because they were still kneecapping each other at the time, and another one was sold out in Madrid and when we arrived there the previous night, we went out for dinner and afterwards they told us that it had been cancelled because they were afraid that there was going to be trouble. Then one in Mexico City got replaced by one in Canada, at a radio station's private party. When we came out, half the crowd were delighted to see the Sex Pistols and the other half were pissed off because they wanted to see Bachman Turner Overdrive!

I think the role of the bass is to provide a bit of colour, and to float somewhere between the guitar and the drums. That's possibly what's wrong with *Never Mind The Bollocks,...*: some of my bass parts were written to provide a counterpoint between what Steve and Paul were doing. When I did the tour, I tried to make the bass parts less busy than they'd been before, but also supply something that was missing. If it feels right you don't have to concentrate too much. We've played together for so long, we know what feels right. The only time you notice when something is wrong, is when it's wrong! There weren't any cock-ups as far as the band were concerned, although John sometimes comes in at different times in the song and we turn a bar or half a bar around with a nod and a wink between me, Steve and Paul. We did a lot of that. But that happens in bands.

It was at the Phoenix festival where John got squirted with paint by one of Chumbawamba, which wasn't a cool thing to do. I don't know what their problem was. It didn't half make John angry.

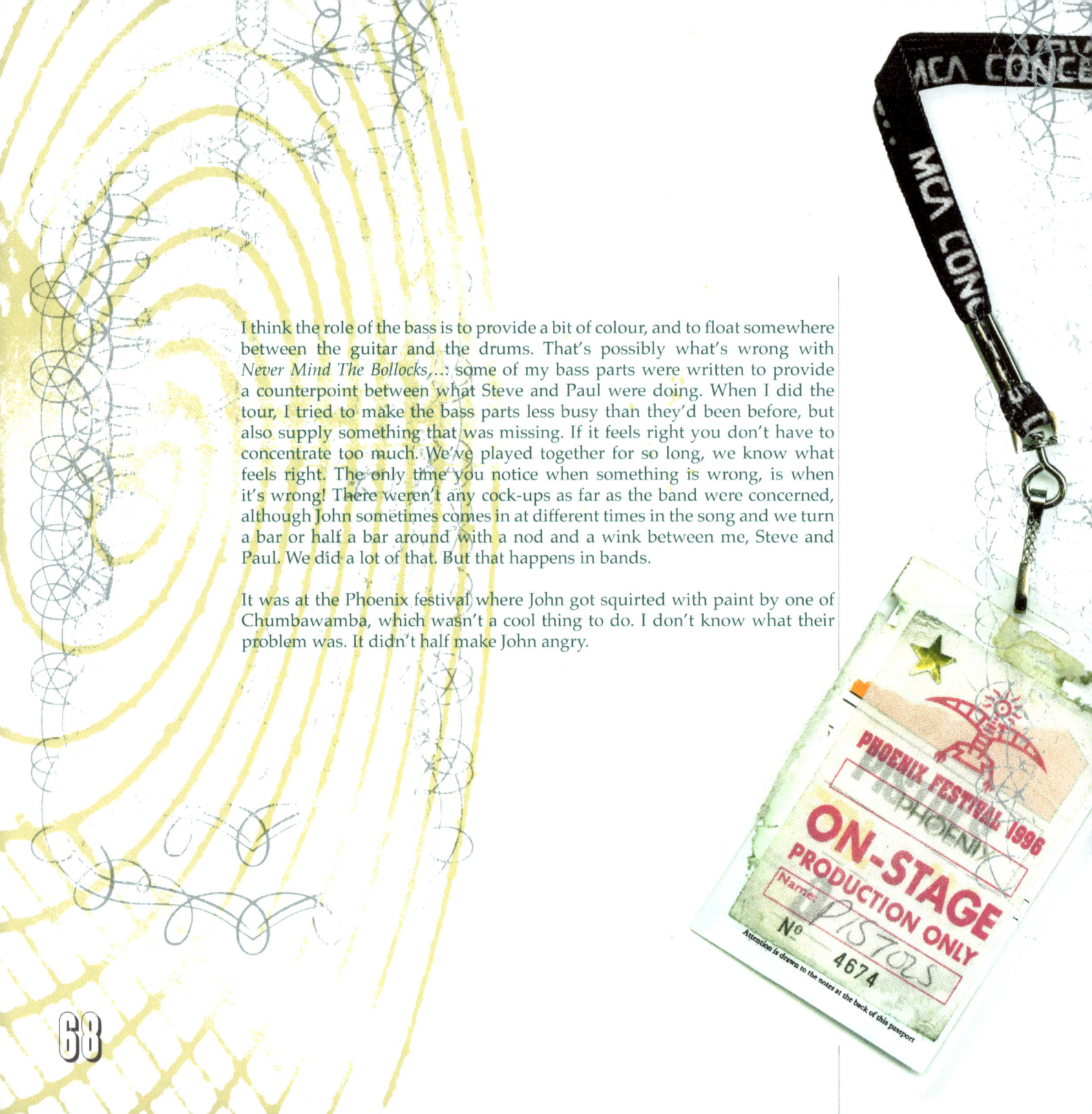

Between legs of the tour I went to Corsica, and very nice it was too. I thought I'd grow a moustache, I'm not sure why: I might have had a pimple or something, and I didn't want to shave it! Then I had a beard. But you grow a beard and then you trim it too much on one side, and then you do the other one, and it ends up getting smaller and smaller.

31 July Red Rocks Amphitheater, Denver 2 August Music Complex, Dallas 3 August International Ballroom, Houston 4 August Mud Island Amphitheater, Memphis 6 August Patriot Center, Fairfax, Washington 8 August Roseland Ballroom, New York 9 August Roseland Ballroom, New York 10 August Great Woods Centre, Boston 12 August Molson Amphitheater, Toronto, Canada 13 August Nautica Stage, Cleveland 14 August Iclight Amphitheater, Pittsburgh (cancelled) 16 August Cobo Arena, Detroit 17 August Aragon Ballroom, Chicago 18 August Eagles Ballroom, Milwaukee 20 August Sports Palace, Mexico City, Mexico (cancelled) 20 August Goverment Entertainment Complex, Toronto, Canada 22 August MCA Universal Amphitheater, Los Angeles 23 August Hollywood Palladium, Los Angeles 25 August Hollywood Palladium, Los Angeles 27 August Shoreline Amphitheater, Mountain View 29 August Civic Auditorium, Portland 30 August Bumpershoots Festival, Seattle 31 August Pacific National Exhibition Center, Vancouver, Canada

12

31 JULY	RED ROCKS AMPHITHEATER, DENVER
2 AUGUST	MUSIC COMPLEX, DALLAS
3 AUGUST	INTERNATIONAL BALLROOM, HOUSTON
4 AUGUST	MUD ISLAND AMPHITHEATER, MEMPHIS
6 AUGUST	PATRIOT CENTER, FAIRFAX, WASHINGTON
8 AUGUST	ROSELAND BALLROOM, NEW YORK
9 AUGUST	ROSELAND BALLROOM, NEW YORK
10 AUGUST	GREAT WOODS CENTRE, BOSTON
12 AUGUST	MOLSON AMPHITHEATER, TORONTO, CANADA
13 AUGUST	NAUTICA STAGE, CLEVELAND
16 AUGUST	COBA ARENA, DETROIT
17 AUGUST	ARAGON BALLROOM, CHICAGO
18 AUGUST	EAGLES BALLROOM, MILWAUKEE
20 AUGUST	GUVERMENT ENTERTAINMENT COMPLEX, TORONTO, CANADA
22 AUGUST	MCA UNIVERSAL AMPHITHEATER, LOS ANGELES
23 AUGUST	HOLLYWOOD PALLADIUM, LOS ANGELES
25 AUGUST	HOLLYWOOD PALLADIUM, LOS ANGELES
27 AUGUST	SHORELINE AMPHITHEATER, MOUNTAIN VIEW
29 AUGUST	CIVIC AUDITORIUM, PORTLAND
30 AUGUST	BUMPERSHOOTS FESTIVAL, SEATTLE
31 AUGUST	PACIFIC NATIONAL EXHIBITION CENTER, VANCOUVER, CANADA

NORTH AMERICA

Memorabilia from America. I spent a lot of time in the health club in the Watergate Hotel. It'd be a lot more expensive than that nowadays...

What a young blade! I was either 39 or 40 in that picture. We started the tour with a stylist, but he was rubbish so we ended up going shopping ourselves. You know what's you and what isn't.

I was quite pleased with that shirt: I bought it in New York. I looked at it, and it should have been 190 dollars, but it was reduced to 19 in the sale. When I was out shopping I bumped into Steve and I said 'Where are you off to?' and he said, 'Well, if you wait for everyone else you never get anything done,' and I said 'I know, I've already done it, Steve'. Everyone gets on top of each other. I've never been one for sitting and watching TV, especially daytime TV: you might as well go out.

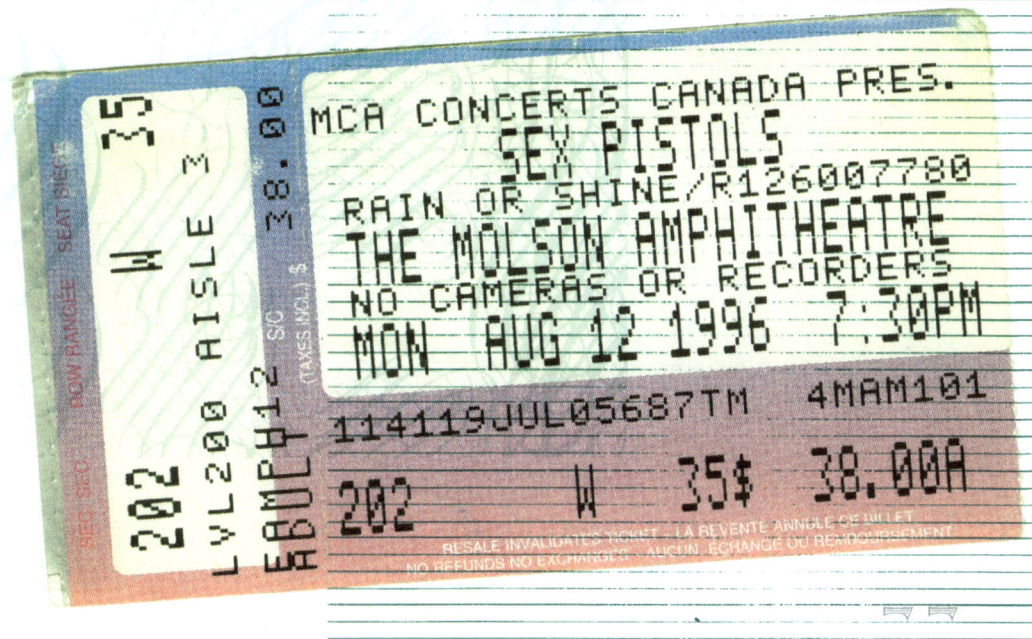

My cheque for appearing on the Letterman show. A mighty 22 dollars and 37 cents. I've never cashed it. Why would I? It's more fun to hang on to as a souvenir.

> "The greatest band in the history of the world." It's not a bad thing to have said about you, but that's not what he's actually saying, the bastard! He thinks we let them down badly. The end of the review isn't there, but we can write our own.

Forever Rotten

The Sex Pistols Reunion
Finsbury Park
June 23

BY ROBERT CHRISTGAU

The deal was, if I would interview this band I like named Fluffy for *Spin*, their label would transport me to London, where Fluffy was opening for the Sex Pistols at a place called Finsbury Park on June 23. Now, as someone whose impulse was to skip the Pistols' revolting reunion even if John Lydon rang me up and begged, I should in theory have been tempted by this offer. But I was — not because Iggy would be there too, not because after 29 years as a rock critic it was about time I got to weekend in London, but because... well, because the perversity of the concept appealed to me. What better reason to catch the motherfuckers than because they were sharing a bill with Fluffy? So at the last minute I decided to take a flier.

Of the many things I didn't know about this gig going in, two loom large. No one could have comprehended that England would upset Spain in the European Football Championships the day before. But the other I should have had a bead on: Finsbury Park is where John Lydon grew up. In the standard texts — Fred and Judy Vermorel, Greil Marcus, even Jon Savage — little or nothing is made of this. The emphasis is on Lydon's rootlessness, a radical alienation that Marcus traces back to the dawn of the millennium. But Lydon's autobiography, *Rotten: No Irish, No Blacks, No Dogs*, which I wolfed down on the plane back, devotes almost 70 engaged, pungent pages to a childhood experienced mostly in that working-class North London neighborhood, where Irish battled English and, if they had any sense, befriended Jamaicans. Lydon is cynical about his working-class compatriots, who he considers "downtrodden" by their own passivity: "We're lazy, good-for-nothing bastards, absolute cop-outs." And he's never gushy about his strong, broad-minded, eccentric family — his mother beset by illness, introspective yet a rock, delighted by his Stooges and Hawkwind records; his father responsible, distant, his theory of nurturance limited to instilling his own toughness in his four sons. But the Man Who Can Be Rotten is proud of his roots nevertheless. He's been tight with his dad ever since his mother died in 1979. And as far as he's concerned, it was his Finsbury Park gang, including future teachers and craftsmen who are still his friends, who created the sensibility usually credited to Malcolm McLaren and the band he managed.

Lydon has despised McLaren forever, and although who invented punk would be a stumper even without their feud, it would be foolish to base any conclusions on his say-so. Nevertheless, I've long felt that of these two guys I wouldn't want my sister to marry, Lydon is the errant genius with his head up his ass, McLaren the wack poseur with hair on his palms. It's plain enough that the Sex Pistols — and the movement they inspired, which Lydon, typically, disavows for its conformism and pub-rock taint — needed both of them. But I go along with what the courts eventually decided: Lydon deserves the patent. When it's Svengalis against performers, performers usually do, and without doubt Lydon gave shape to what was only McLaren's half-cocked fantasy. God knows what McLaren's Sex Pistols reunion would have been like — some fashion show in disguise, with faux-satirical attention to the genteel accoutrements Malc can't live with and can't live without. At least the comeback tour announced by Lydon, Steve Jones, Paul Cook, and Lydon's old antagonist Glen Matlock couldn't be any worse than Kiss or the Doobie Brothers.

Only of course it could. Kiss are crass by definition, the Doobies mushheads, and since nostalgia is crass and mushy, there's a fit there. Punk nostalgia, on the other hand, is a grotesque oxymoron. What can it mean to pine for a time when you were young and nihilistic? To look back 20 years to when you believed there was no future? The answers to these questions are not pretty: electric Luddism, "Live Music Is Better" bumper stickers, dress codes, chauvinism, disco sucks in a dozen guises, the censure of any pleasure not your miserable own. Add to these resentments the location of John Lydon's head as he heaped obloquy on his fans and denied that he had anything to do with rock and roll, and you have a formula for the most tedious kind of ritual abuse. The only mystery was the exact form of the ensuing travesty. Would it be a rote replay of songs that had long since failed to dent the system they railed against? Or a wandering stop-and-go in which the musicians bollocksed their cues and cursed each other out as Lydon explained to the paying customers how stupid they'd been to show up?

Well, neither. What I forgot until I got to London was that in the U.S. the Pistols were subculture exotica, while in Britain they were a native-grown mass phenomenon. To the amusement of the British press, which instantly declared the Pistols over because they were over, Finsbury Park wasn't just a concert — it was an all-Sunday festival that upped its draw by advertising nine bands old and new. And draw it did, albeit not like Kiss at the Garden crowded for the Buzzcocks at four, it had spilled a near-capacity 28,000 £22.50 ticket-holders across the grass by the time Iggy appeared at 7:25. Although the spike-headed thirtysomethings with baby buggies made for eye-catching photoplay, the age range of this very male (and very white) crowd was wide, say 17 to 43, and amazingly, the generational spread was almost even, tilted only a tad toward the older end. But because 1977's art-punks and their techno heirs were too smart to waste time on over-because-it's-over, it was uniform in another respect: class. These were the blokes who had stuck with punk long after Johnny Rotten threw in the towel, yelling along loudest when the P.A. blasted Sham 69's "Hersham Boys." The dominant style of the support bands wasn't Fluffy's minimalism of necessity but the expansive pop oi that linked veteran campaigners Stiff Little Fingers, still at it 17 years after "Alternative Ulster," and "Suspect Device," to the hook-seeking 60 Ft Dolls and big-rock Wildhearts: guitar-bassanddrums, unison vocals and catchy terrace chants, fast martial rhythms shading or switching into thrash.

Dress was rough but sharp, with a tiny minority in costume and vintage T's scattered among the new souvenirs. There was some pogoing by oldtimers contesting their mortality, spotty moshing, and no gobbing at all; especially given how much alcohol was around, the jovial concord with which stumblers were righted and shutterbugs mounted strangers' shoulders seemed utopian. And from what I could gather, the genial mood wasn't just I-have-survived. A vast majority of those present were into soccer, and England's victory on Saturday had put them in the full flush of the symbolic chauvinism only sports fans can wallow in. God fuck the queen and save Stuart Pearce, an old punk who'd saved the day with a penalty kick against Spain after ignominiously blowing a World Cup match six years before.

Although all this is easy enough to figure out in retrospect, at Finsbury Park it had to sneak up on me. Jet lag, uneven music, yet somehow I was having a lovely time. The Buzzcocks got singalong like Pete Seeger, Skunk Anansie put me to sleep, the Wildhearts set off their smoke machine, and then I was holding my ground at my first Iggy

Fucking fit: the "lazy, good-for-nothing bastard" onstage

show since the '70s. I've never bought James Osterberg's self-made legend, but at 49 he was every bit as pumped as I'd been hearing. Dry-fucking the amps, jacking a rocket-sized imaginary hard-on, parading his sinewy torso and shaking his skinny ass, bodysurfing into the crowd to throw a punch or two, he wasted no ceremony getting to "Raw Power," "Search and Destroy," and "I Wanna Be Your Dog," and he never let up. "He's fucking fit, man," noted one fit student of the arts. "He's fucking fit," his mate responded. How did John propose to follow this?

Yet when the moment came it wasn't even an issue. After a 45-minute interval, guitaristbassistanddrummer took the stage and Rotten burst through a scrim of 1977 shock-horror headlines in a shiny laminated-linen suit, windowpane plaid with ridiculous shoulder pads. In an instant the crowd, which had only tightened seriously with Iggy, transformed itself into a roiling mass, an exuberantly physical yet far from hostile pogo pit. And suddenly it was clear that to the last Iggyite these people were there for one reason and one reason only: to see the greatest band in the history of the world.

The Pistols had changed the over-30s' lives with a few records and some phantom gigs; the kids had read about the same band in the first chapter of Genesis, shining light on the face of the

CONTINUED ON PAGE 52

MUSIC

AND SUDDENLY it was clear that to the last Iggyite these people were there for one reason and one reason only: to see ==the greatest band in the history of the world.==

ALSO IN THIS SECTION
NAS
JAY-Z
LINCOLN CENTER FESTIVAL '96

A parody of punk? Yeah right. *What's new?*, was my reaction to that kind of thing. It didn't bother us. Steve was always more interested in how many column inches we'd got.

I enjoyed North America. There was a guy in Portland, Oregon who had been on the first Pistols tour of America. I didn't know him: he said hello to me but he was confused. He obviously thought that I'd been on that tour, which I wasn't, obviously. He said he worked for Bill Graham or someone and he said, 'So what have you been doing?' and I said, 'I've been catching up on a bit of reading: since I'm on the road, I thought I'd re-read *On The Road* by Jack Kerouac. It's cool because we were in San Francisco before we came to Portland, where the beatnik movement started.' He said, 'Actually, the beatnik movement was big in San Francisco, but it didn't start there: what happened was, all the free-thinking people from New York went to San Francisco University, and so did some people from Portland – but in 1956, when the beatnik scene started, it was a really hot year, and we had a plague of fleas in Portland. People got out of town and went to San Francisco to escape the fleas, and that's where you'd have Jack Kerouac bumping into

Allen Ginsberg and people like that.' I got this compilation of songs from the beat movement there, and on it there was a copy of 'Beat Generation' by Bob McFadden & Dor, which inspired Richard Hell to write 'Blank Generation'. It was taking the mickey out of the beatniks. "Some people like to rock / Some people like to roll…"

We played the *Letterman Show* on 9 August 1996. The house band plays through the adverts, not just at the end and the beginning of each section of the show, and just before us, they played 'London Calling', which made some sense but didn't go down well with John. It seemed that John knew the bandleader anyway, because his manager at the time also managed him. It was freezing cold in the studio, even though it was the summer: you could see your breath coming out of your mouth. Letterman reckons that people laugh more when they're cold.

We'd watched *Up In Smoke*, the Cheech & Chong film, on video on the bus the night we drove in, and we were sitting in our freezing dressing room, waiting to get called and trying to keep warm, and the door opened and Cheech Marin stuck his head inside. It turned out that he too was managed by John's manager.

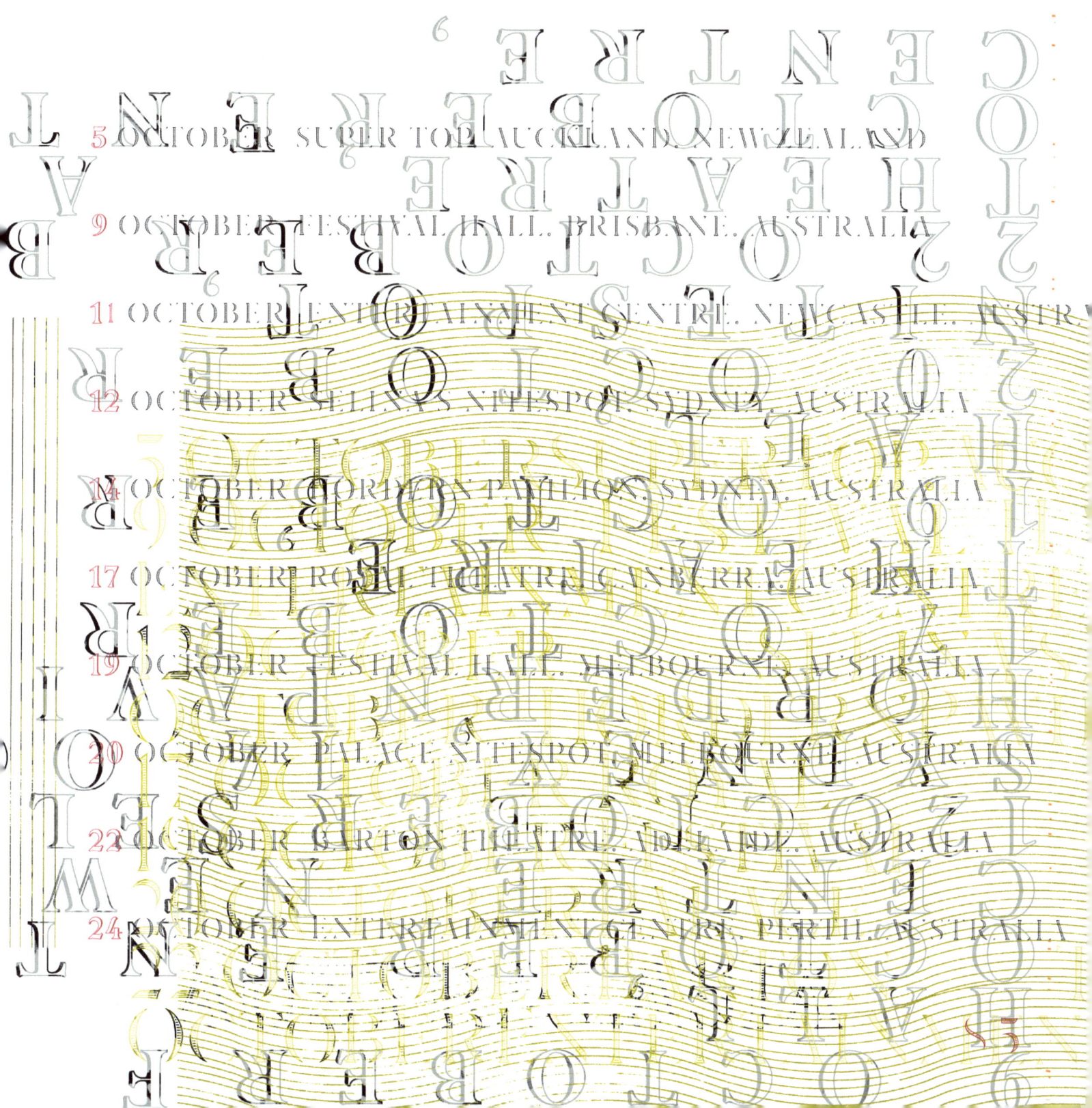

5 OCTOBER SUPER TOP AUCKLAND NEW ZEALAND
9 OCTOBER FESTIVAL HALL BRISBANE AUSTRALIA
11 OCTOBER ENTERTAINMENT CENTRE NEWCASTLE AUSTRALIA
12 OCTOBER SELINAS NITESPOT SYDNEY AUSTRALIA
14 OCTOBER HORDERN PAVILION SYDNEY AUSTRALIA
17 OCTOBER ROYAL THEATRE CANBERRA AUSTRALIA
19 OCTOBER FESTIVAL HALL MELBOURNE AUSTRALIA
20 OCTOBER PALACE NITESPOT MELBOURNE AUSTRALIA
22 OCTOBER BARTON THEATRE ADELAIDE AUSTRALIA
24 OCTOBER ENTERTAINMENT CENTRE PERTH AUSTRALIA

When we were in Australia, the record company proudly gave us all the press they'd set up for us. You don't normally read all this stuff, but I was flicking through the magazines and found an interview that Steve had done about his other band, the Neurotic Outsiders. Steve said in this interview, 'I much prefer singing in the Neurotic Outsiders because you've got no big egos to worry about, because we all play instruments' – which is true: there's always a difference between a singer who plays and a singer who doesn't play. They're on different pages. He didn't bad-mouth John, but there was something there, and for the whole time we were in Australia – three weeks or whatever – John didn't mention it. We all knew that John had read it: it was the elephant in the room, until it finally exploded. I wasn't involved with it, but it was funny. Normal musicians just get on with it, but John plays a game: it's like playing chess with him. I think life's too short for that, myself.

I've got friends in Sydney so I hung out with them. I went over to Manly with my ex-wife and her young kid. It was quite touching, actually: he was about six or seven at the time. I had him on my shoulders and he said, 'Do you know what, Glen? You're the best friend I've ever had.'

SEX PISTOLS
NEW ZEALAND, AUSTRALIA, JAPAN, SOUTH AMERICAN TOUR 1996
SCHEDULE AT-A-GLANCE

DATE	CITY	VENUE
SEPT.		
MON 30	LONDON/LAX	
OCTOBER		
TUE 01		FLY TO AUCKLAND
WED 02	MID-AIR!	
THU 03	AUCKLAND, NZ	
FRI 04	AUCKLAND, NZ	
SAT 05	AUCKLAND, NZ	
SUN 06	AUCKLAND, NZ	MID-AIR!
MON 07	SYDNEY, AUS	OFF
TUE 08	SYDNEY, AUS	PROD. R'HAL
WED 09	SYDNEY, AUS	SUPER TOP
THU 10	BRISBANE, AUS	OFF
FRI 11	SYDNEY, AUS	PRESS CONFERENCE
SAT 12	NEWCASTLE, AUS	FESTIVAL HALL
SUN 13	SYDNEY, AUS	OFF
MON 14	SYDNEY, AUS	ENT. CENTRE
TUE 15	SYDNEY, AUS	OFF
WED 16	SYDNEY, AUS	OFF
THU 17	SYDNEY, AUS	HORDERN PAVILION
FRI 18	CANBERRA, AUS	*SELINAS
SAT 19	MELBOURNE, AUS	OFF
SUN 20	MELBOURNE, AUS	ROYAL THEATRE
MON 21	MELBOURNE, AUS	OFF
TUE 22	ADELAIDE, AUS	FESTIVAL HALL
WED 23	ADELAIDE, AUS	*PALACE THEATER
THU 24	PERTH, AUS	OFF
FRI 25	PERTH, AUS	THEBARTON THEATRE
SAT 26	MID-AIR	OFF
SUN 27	TOKYO, JAPAN	ENT. CENTRE
MON 28	TOKYO, JAPAN.	FLY TO TOKYO
TUE 29	TOKYO, JAPAN	OFF
WED 30	OSAKA, JAPAN	CLUB CITTA
THU 31	OSAKA, JAPAN	CLUB CITTA
		OFF
		I.M.P. HALL

* GIGS ARE NOT CONFIRMED - PROBABLY WON'T HAPPEN.

The staff of Virgin in Australia gave us these little welcome cards, which was nice, I thought. And there's my round-the-world ticket, with the paper copy in pink print that you always used to get back then. People were generally friendly to us, we found.

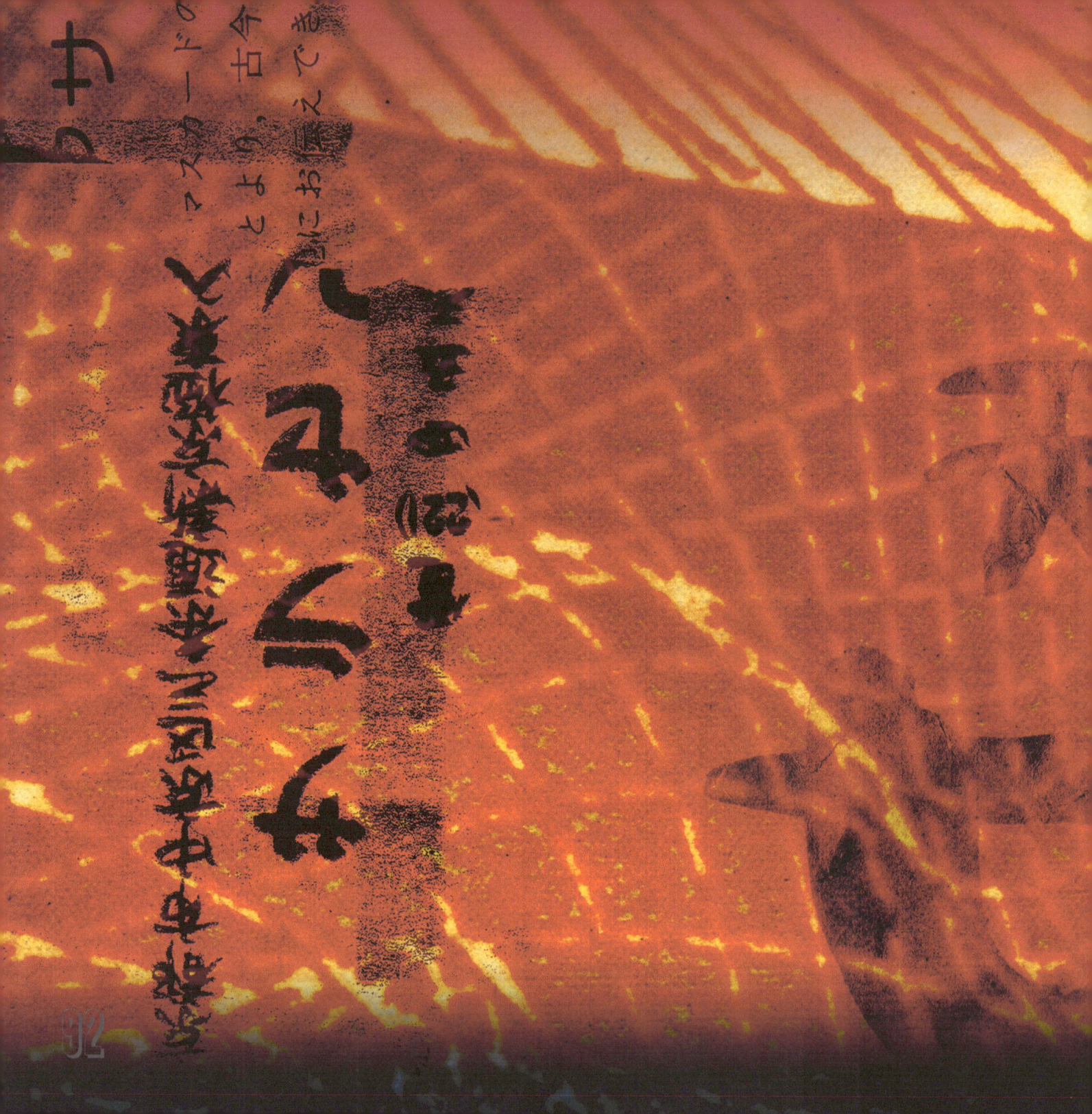

28 OCTOBER   CLUB CITTA KANAGAWA, KAWASAKI
29 OCTOBER   CLUB CITTA KANAGAWA, KAWASAKI
31 OCTOBER   IMPERIAL HALL, OSAKA
1 NOVEMBER   IMPERIAL HALL, OSAKA
2 NOVEMBER   IMPERIAL HALL, OSAKA
4 NOVEMBER   NIPPON BUDOKAN, TOKYO
5 NOVEMBER   NIPPON BUDOKAN, TOKYO
7 NOVEMBER   SUN PALACE, FUKUOKA
9 NOVEMBER   DIAMOND HALL, NAGOYA
10 NOVEMBER DIAMOND HALL, NAGOYA
11 NOVEMBER DIAMOND HALL, NAGOYA
13 NOVEMBER IMPERIAL HALL, OSAKA
14 NOVEMBER IMPERIAL HALL, OSAKA
16 NOVEMBER NIPPON BUDOKAN, TOKYO
17 NOVEMBER SYAKAIBUNKA KAIKAN, MATSUMOTO
19 NOVEMBER CLUB CITTA KANAGAWA, KAWASAKI
21 NOVEMBER HOKKAIDO KOUSEINENKIN KAIKAN, SAPPORO
23 NOVEMBER SUN PLAZA HALL, SENDAI

Japan was different to the rest of the tour, somehow. They looked after us, although the food was a bit much at times. When in Rome, as Paul told me.

Before we went to Japan, I told my dad that we were playing at the Budokan in Tokyo and said, 'You won't have heard of it' – but he had done, because he used to do judo and it's the headquarters of all the martial arts, which I never knew. It's a bit lacking in atmosphere there, though, because it's considered sacred. It's quasi-religious. When you play in Japan, everyone in the crowd goes 'Wa-hey!' for a couple of seconds after each song, and then there's total silence. It's a bit disconcerting. You're wondering 'Did that go down well, or not?' I said to one of them afterwards, 'How come you don't make any noise between numbers? In any other country in the world, they shout things out,' and he said, 'Yes, but that is silly, because you are English and we are Japanese and you wouldn't understand us.' I thought 'Try telling that to a German or a Spaniard.' Anyway, it's a measure of where they're at, somehow. At other shows it was totally different: they were all trying to stage-dive.

The audiences were all quite young, although it was difficult to tell because they all looked fairly sprightly: they ranged from teenagers to people in their 40s. Touring over there was an excuse to see some friends: one of them was Morgan Fisher, who used to be in Mott The Hoople. He came to the Budokan. Another memory of that venue: I was on an internal flight with Steve, and I noticed that he was smirking. I said, 'What's going on?' and he said, 'That air hostess fancies you.' She was very fit, so I got talking to her and invited her to the gig. I didn't think much of it, but when I was at the venue, all of a sudden this massive bunch of flowers arrived. Steve automatically assumed they were for him, but they weren't: they were for me, from her.

JAPAN

This is a friend of mine, Yuko, who I'd got to know over the years. Japanese people always give you presents. They're generally pretty friendly. Some of them dress quite wackily, but they're mostly very polite and deferential.

I've kept those cigarettes for all these years — and there's a bag of chestnuts which I bought in the street. We would have been lost without those street maps: because Steve and I weren't drinking, we spent a lot of time exploring and seeing the sights. One obvious benefit of being sober.

We don't look bad, do we? I've no idea where this is: it might be the Budokan. I wasn't involved in any of the practical side of the tours: fuck that! We did pay for it, though: it all comes out of your winnings, doesn't it? The tour manager was a guy called Frankie Enfield, who did a very good job. There was also a guy who looked after the band and another one who looked after the equipment. They were a good crew.

Smash were the Japanese promoters. They were very good: we did the Fiji festival with them. Backstage various things would go on: sometimes there would be a meet and greet, but it was quite businesslike really. Mates would come back. Paul would have a quiet drink, John would have a loud one, me and Steve were on the wagon. I'd been sober for a good 10 years before this.

With fans next to the equipment truck. It was huge. Smash Corporation were the local promoters and they took care of us, even giving us a night in a ryokan, a traditional guest house, at the end of the tour.

A Pistols album of some kind is advertised on this flyer — but no-one could tell us what it was. We didn't know if it was a live album, a reissue, a bootleg, or what, and we still don't know all these years later. If you're reading this and you know what it was, get in touch!

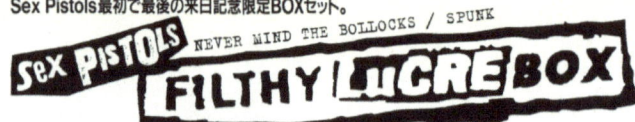

It was fantastic travelling the world first class and playing for lots of people, and it was also fantastic to reclaim my part and to earn some proper money for the first time. Touring is a lot of hanging around, though, and of course there's the jet lag. It's not the hour on stage that is the problem, it's the 23 hours hanging about. It was a mixture of emotions, and everyone was still skirting around each other a bit.

I remember flying from Australia to Japan, and they'd given us some pre-press stuff that had come out. You know those little Japanese rock magazines? In the small ads there was an advert, possibly for the live album or possibly for a bootleg, and the text said 'Live At The Budokan', advertising a record. I never saw the finished thing.

We were always on the fucking bullet train. What happened was, we did these three initial shows, and then there was a big demand for us, so the next shows weren't necessarily in geographical order. The first time we were like, 'Here we go, Mount Fuji' and then you go to Tokyo and then you go back again and it's like, fucking hell! And all the time we were being given 50 things and being asked to sign them.

There was some girl who, when we were flying from Japan to Australia, gave the stewardess a note to give to me. I thought 'This is interesting' and put her on the guest list every night in Japan, because she was making the effort to come, and most people aren't nutters after all. She seemed all right, but we found out later that she was a nutcase. She accused one of the roadies of raping her, and the Japanese police got involved: they came to protect us from her.

When you tour properly, you get treated properly. As long as everybody's making money, everybody's happy. If you needed something, it would be got for you, although it didn't necessarily happen immediately when we were in Japan. You had to have a meeting about everything. They don't seem to have a word for 'No'. We'd ask if we could have something and they'd say, 'Yes, you can't have it!' Even if it was something small like your laundry: you'd ask if it could be done, and it would take so long that it was quicker to go and do it yourself.

In the dressing rooms it was just us, but we did a lot of meet and greets. That's the name of the game. They can be tedious, but it all depends what your attitude is. Mine was just to do it, and keep everybody happy. I used to just show my face and then fuck off.

John and his minder Rambo at the bullet train station. we went everywhere by bullet train, it's an amazing way to travel. In fact, because Japanese gigs kept being added on to the tour itinerary, we found ourselves travelling all over the country more than once, retracing our steps.

FUCKING BULLET TRAIN

Steve looked great: he was really keeping himself fit. We had some great times on that tour, me and him, just because we went around together and made the effort to get out of the hotels and see things.

The dressing room: possibly backstage at the Budokan. There's chips on our rider, look. We were treated well pretty much everywhere.

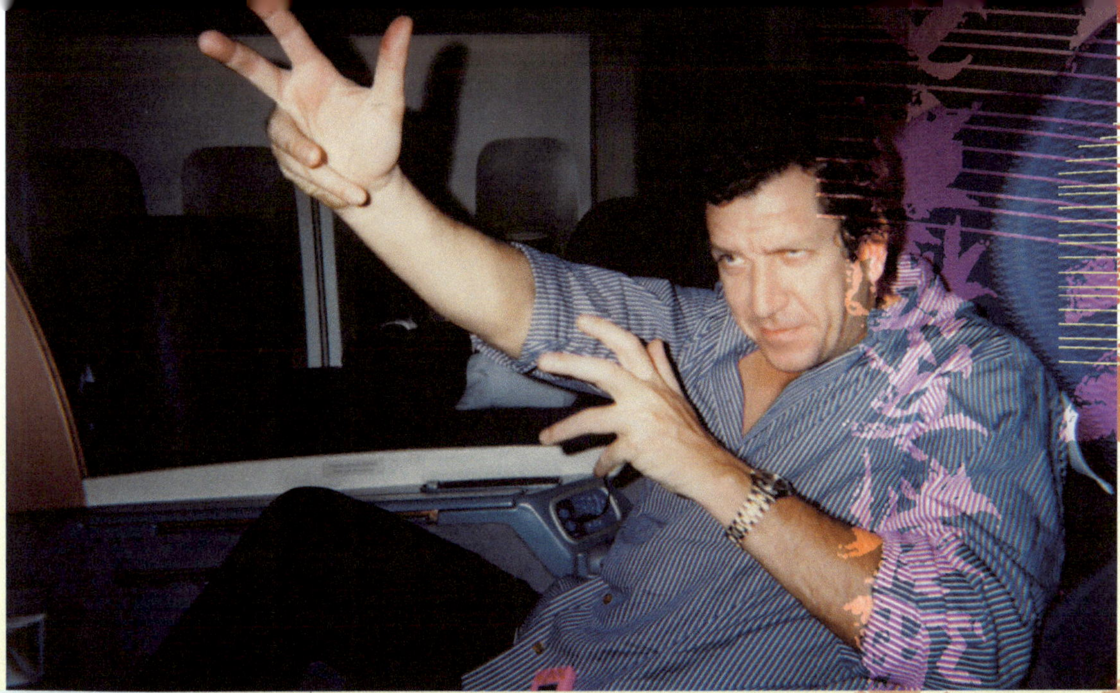

You could smoke on planes then. That was probably a flight from Australia to Japan. I don't really enjoy long-distance travel, although I'm much better now than I was. Was jet lag a problem? Not half. You can't do much about it, though.

Steve was in good shape, and he worked hard to stay that way. We used to go out for walks and explore a bit. Here's a funny story: we were in Osaka, and the hotel was a little way out of town, and there was a river. Over the other side of the river was a castle, like a big shogun kind of building, so we went over there one Saturday morning. We were standing in the quadrangle in the middle of it, and suddenly a Japanese schoolkid started shouting, 'You Glen Matlock! You Glen Matlock! You wait! You wait!' He ran off to the gift shop and came back with a mug with Osaka Castle on it. I don't know if he was trying to tell me something... I've still got it somewhere. As soon as he'd done that, all these other schoolkids started coming up and asking for autographs. That was fine, but then they wanted some more, and some more, and it got a bit daft, so me and Steve were backing off and they were following us! We walked quicker, and they walked quicker, and then we broke into a run – and we're running round the fucking moat. It was like *The Benny Hill Show*. Eventually we got back to the hotel and John said, 'Where you been?' We said, 'We just got chased by all these Japanese schoolkids.'

This is outside the Budokan, taken by Steve: we just wandered up there to take a look. And there we are out for a meal.

We soundchecked on the first leg of each tour, just to check everything was all right, but we didn't do it after that unless something had gone wrong for some reason. The crew did it, because they liked soundchecking. The crew don't like the band around, because then they can have a laugh. Also, you can do a soundcheck which sounds great, and then it sounds shit when you go on stage, and the opposite is true too, so there's really not much point in you doing it if you have a crew who know what they're doing. So we let them get on with it.

Sometimes we'd have press to do, a radio or TV thing, but we were pretty free most of the time. We were gigging most days. We usually did three days on and one day off to give John's voice a break, as is normal when you're in a band. Every flight we had was a night flight, which is all right if you can sleep on planes, but I only slept once on a plane on that tour, which was when we were coming back after the tour had finished. We left Sao Paulo and had some dinner, and the next thing we're coming in to land in Madrid. It takes you a day to get over a flight like that if you haven't slept, and if you're on the wagon you can't use booze to give yourself a second wind.

I've been to a couple of AA meetings. But I find that if I go to a meeting, I want to have a drink, because everybody goes on about how drunk they used to get. I remember going to one in Tokyo, and there were about six people there as well as us. For a laugh, when it came to the point when you're supposed to talk, we sat there with our arms folded and said nothing. They didn't quite know what to make of us.

We had some security blokes on the tour, but it was pointless. These big American guys would hang out with us a bit, but we didn't need them. When we started the tour, we didn't know how it was going to go: we didn't know what the reaction was going to be. As I understand it, what happens when you have a big show like this is that your personal security guys are in charge of the security that the venue provides. They make sure that the security in the venue are cool. We needed security staff at the gigs, of course, but not when we were just hanging out. It was so well done that everybody felt protected.

That's the crew in Nagoya, waiting. There's Alan who was a fantastic sound guy – the only time you know the sound is no good is when someone moans about it. Nobody ever moaned about it once, he was great. I found out later that he had cancer and that he died afterwards. He soldiered through the whole tour, though. He was a lovely bloke.

This is an aquarium that we visited on a day off, with one of the techs.

This is a nice tempura place. I'm drinking iced tea there. I don't drink Coca-Cola because I think it's part of an imperialist plot. No, I'm joking, it's just too sugary for me. But when I went and bought some green tea from a drinks machine, I noticed that it's made under licence by the Coca-Cola Company, so you can't win.

This was in the same place, with the girl who was our translator. You can't go out in Japan without one. She was nice.

With fans and a can of something soft.

A girl who worked for Smash.

This is a girl who followed the band round for all the shows.

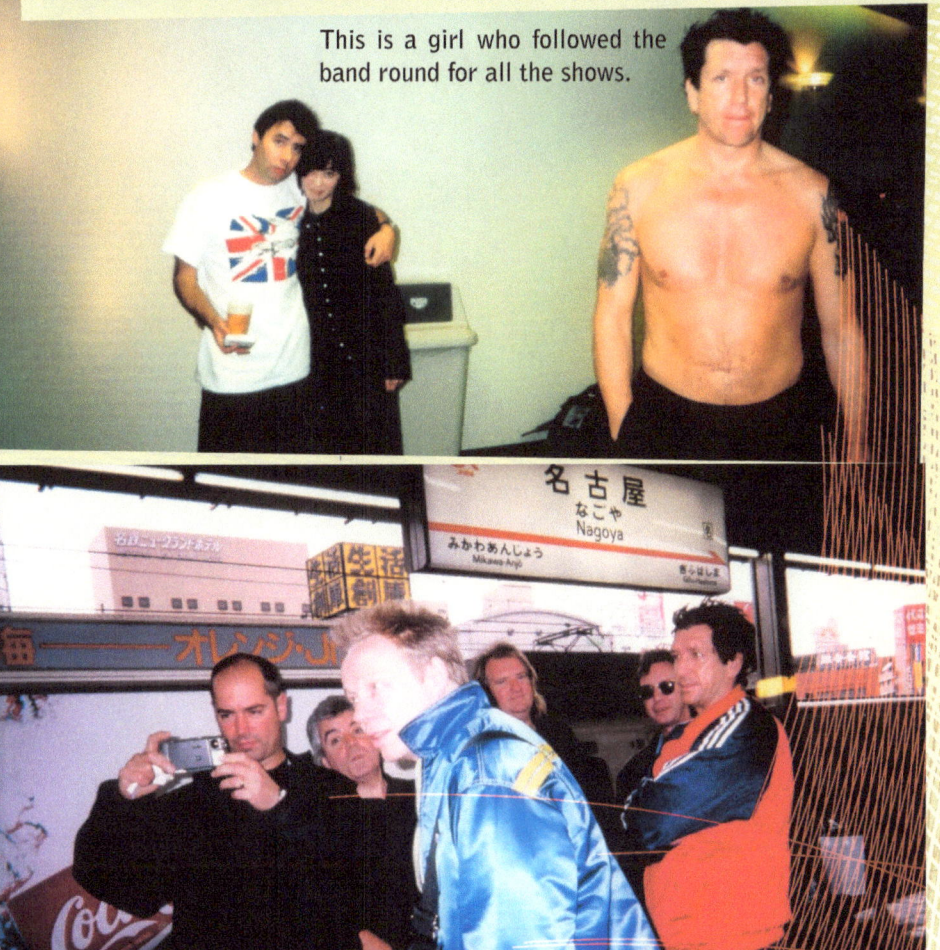

Nagoya. We were waiting for the train and larking about. Mind you, you don't have to wait long for a train in Japan.

John doing his hair. We didn't wear stage make-up or anything, unless we were doing it for a laugh.

Spider crabs are a big delicacy in Japan, and this was the area where they come from.

Those are massage chairs. There was a definite sense that this was all rather surreal, but it's all part of life's rich tapestry.

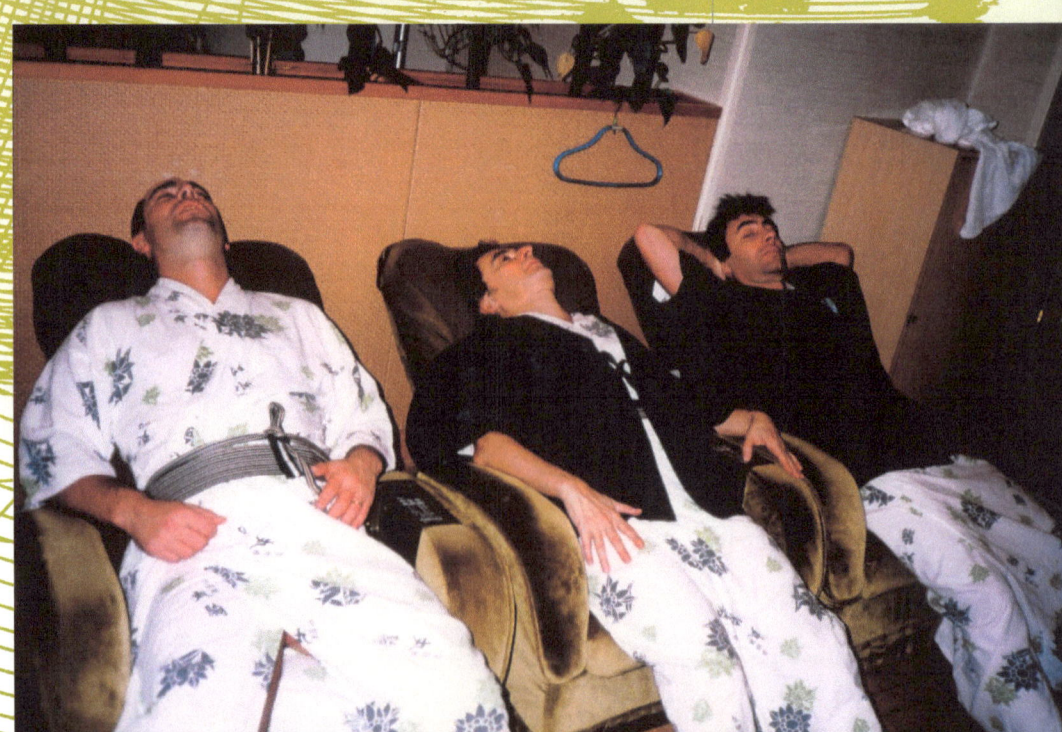

The promoters treated Steve and Paul and me to a night in a ryokan at the end of the tour. A ryokan is a traditional Japanese guesthouse with everybody sleeping on the floor. You have to share a room, and you wear the traditional gear and stay there as long as you like. There was a fantastic lake outside. This was in Sapporo, and it had hot springs. There were monkeys there too. At one point we went outside, because we could hear some singing going on. It was getting louder and louder, and what we saw was a pissed-as-a-fart Japanese businessman and about eight Japanese dolly-birds dressed in Pan Am outfits, with the little hats and stuff, doing all the actions while this bloke was singing 'Michael, Row The Boat Ashore'. It was mad. Very weird.

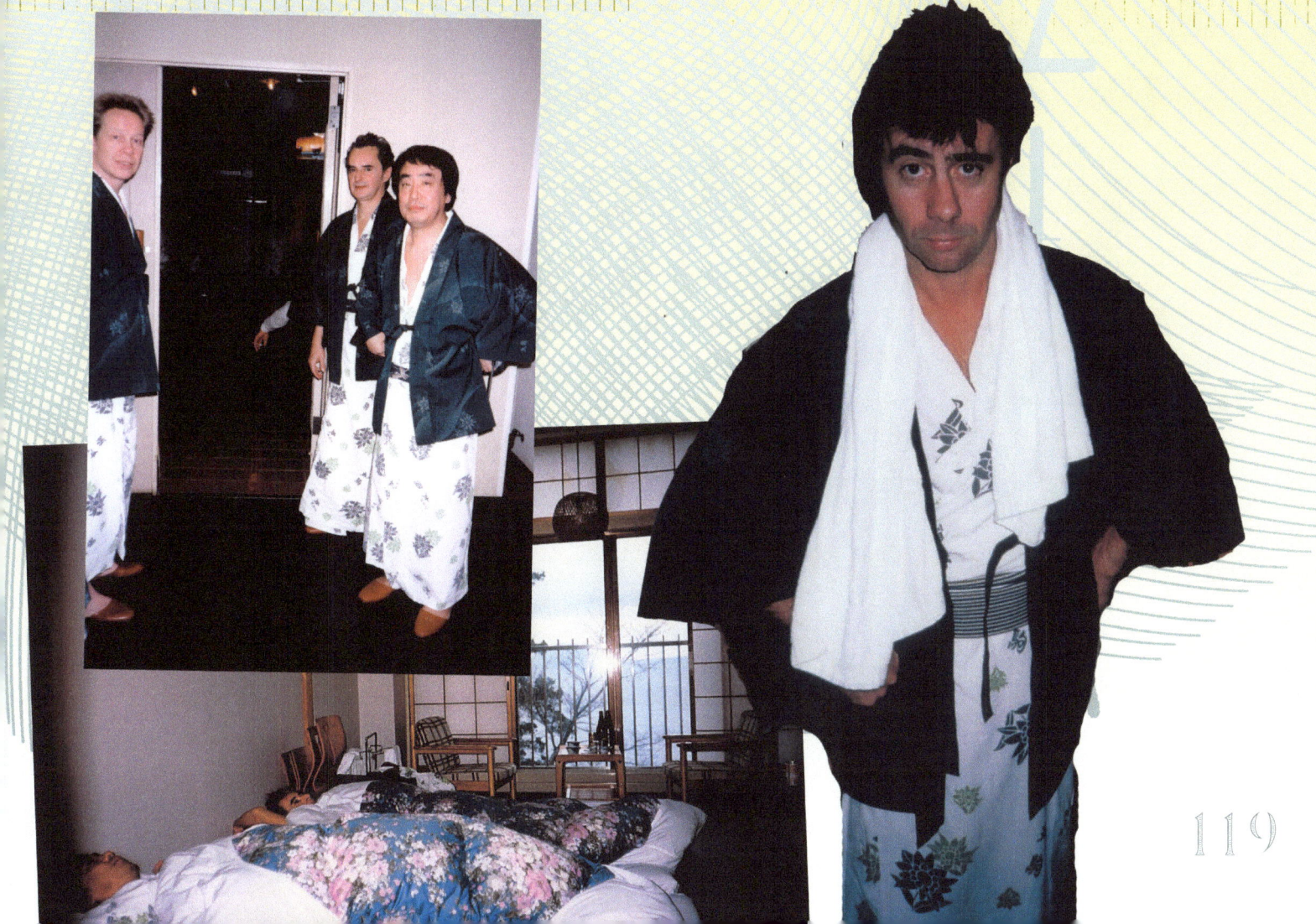

From the lake in Sapporo. The last couple of days in Japan were pretty idyllic. Steve, Paul and I enjoyed the ryokan, although sharing a room was a bit of a pain. There was something about the Japanese that we liked, and they obviously liked us too.

At the samurai monument in Sapporo, where we were chased by fans who wanted to buy us gifts.

Steve and I, the Samurai warriors. I think this shows a slightly different side of the Sex Pistols: we weren't all about aggression.

Steve in a Samurai hairpiece, and John's minder Rambo in a Sumo suit: we were just fooling about backstage.

124

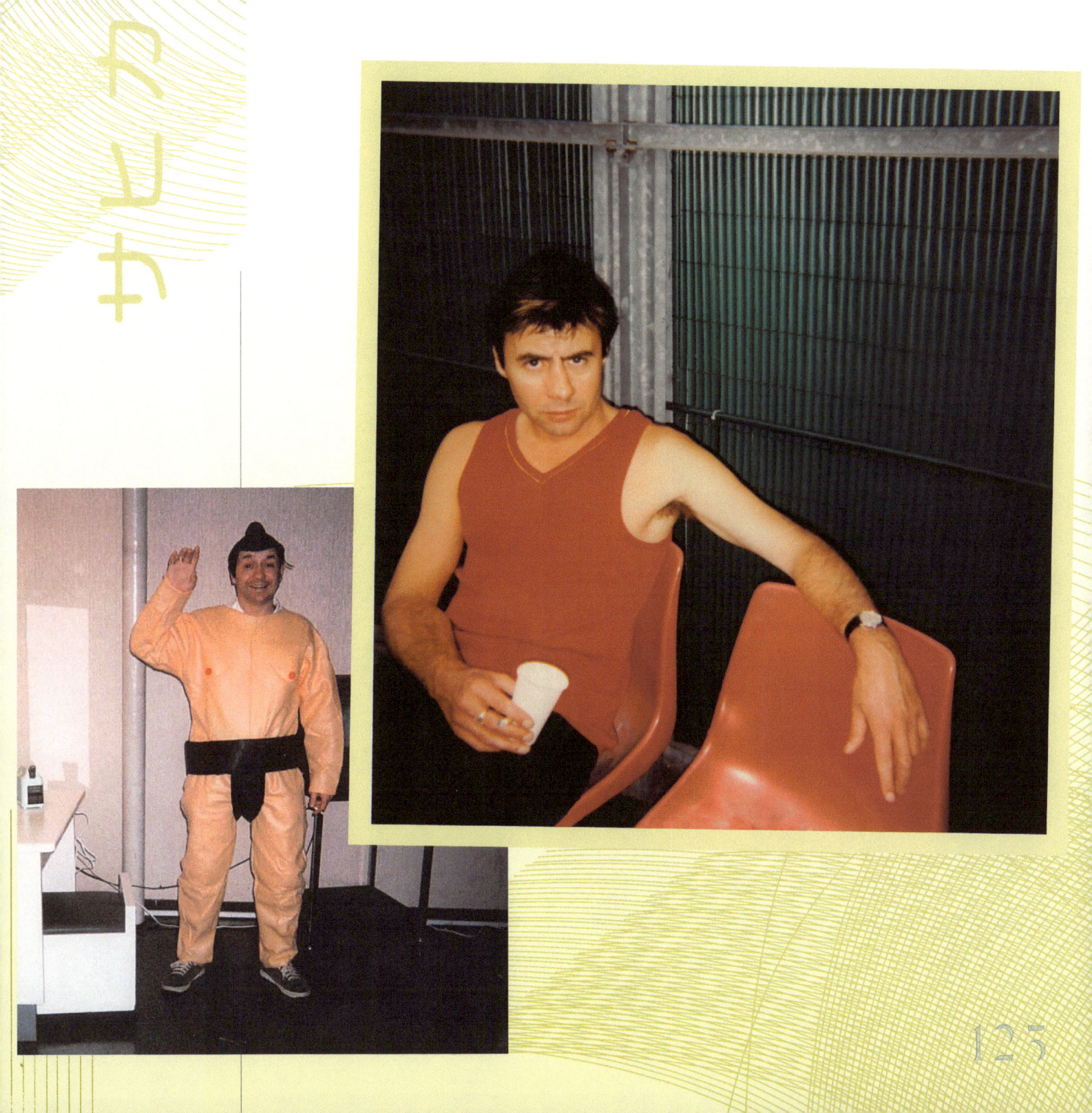

The hats are tourist things made of papier mâché which I bought for the kids. They're supposed to be from a samurai costume.

Out with Paul. I've only ever seen him pissed once. It was at a rehearsal, and he said to me, 'I'm fucking pissed. Take me home!' There was one other time, years ago: we were playing a gig at some college behind Kensington Town Hall and we couldn't find Paul, who had woken up in a rubbish bin.

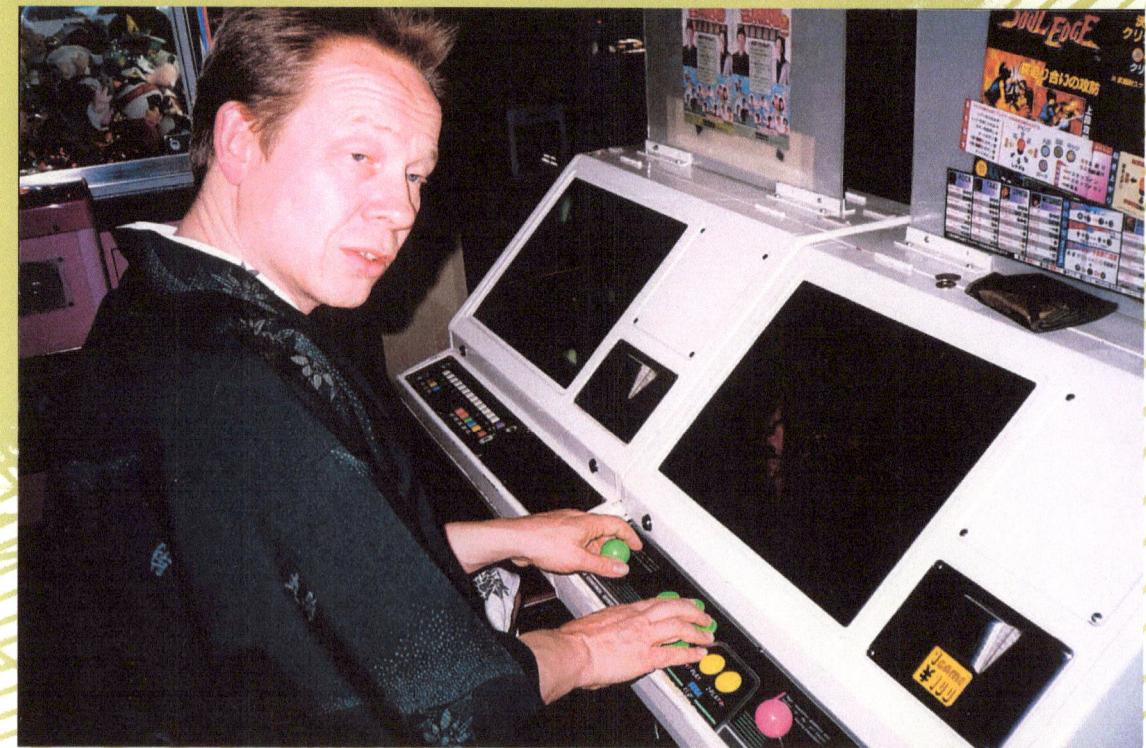

A meal in the ryokan: there were some interesting things on the menu. Am I keen on Japanese food? Well, it kept me going. I'm not really a fan of raw sea cucumber.

This is outside the ryokan: it was beautiful.

This picture of Steve with his old chap on display caused me some grief. Esther Rantzen had started a campaign of some kind about child protection, and on this film there were some pictures of my kids in the bath, plus this picture of Steve. For that reason I said to my missus just before I went away again, 'Don't put those pictures in for developing,' but she put two and two together and made five and thought I'd been up to something on tour with a groupie or something! Anyway, those pictures came back and the guy in Boots was underwhelmed with me: he gave me a look.

JAPAN

The nightlife, although I can't remember where it is. The three of us would go out after soundcheck sometimes, simply because John wasn't needed for that and we'd all be hanging around afterwards. We'd go to a café or something while John was doing press: the journalists wanted to speak to him most, which was normal. It's the same with any band and the lead singer. Steve didn't want to do any press because he hates doing it, but I don't mind doing it myself. In fact I would have liked to do more of it, because it helps build your subsequent career.

A temple in Kyoto. Whenever we went and looked at something, there was invariably a gaggle of schoolkids there.

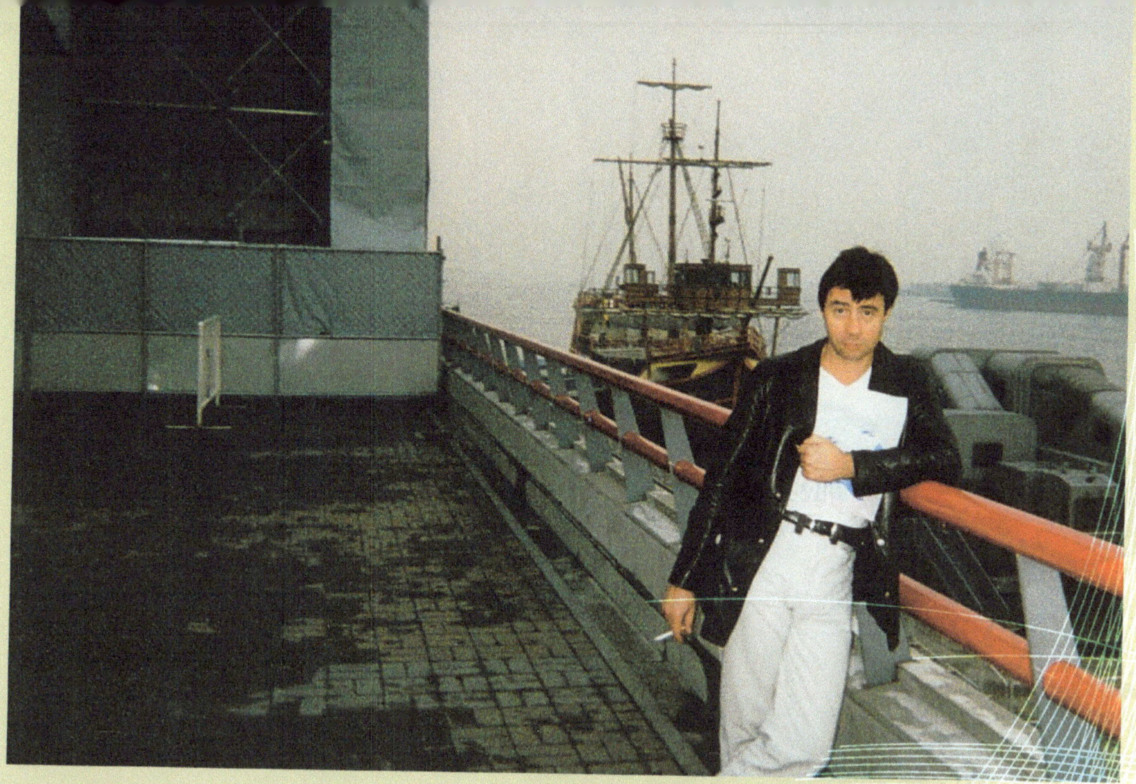

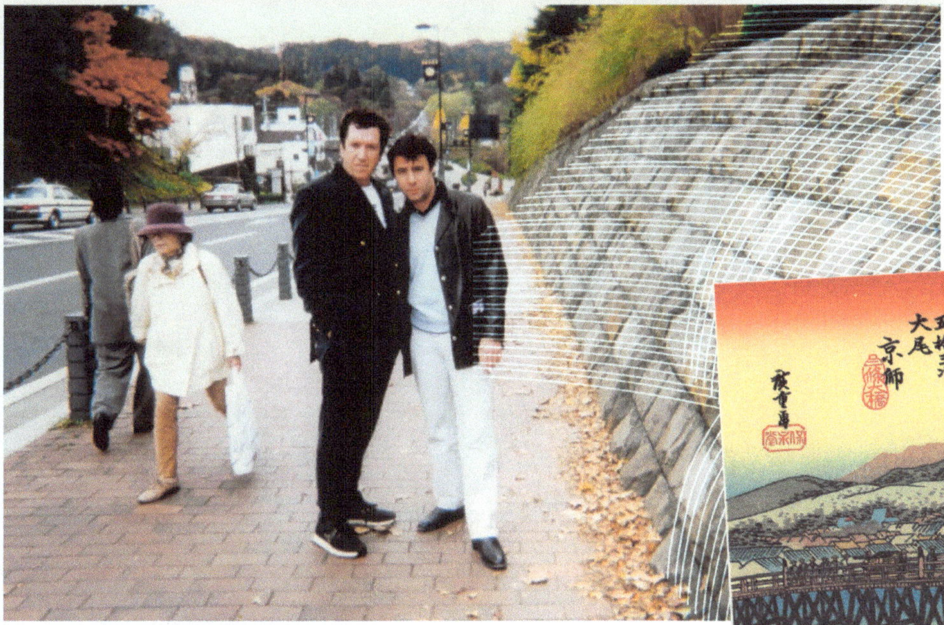

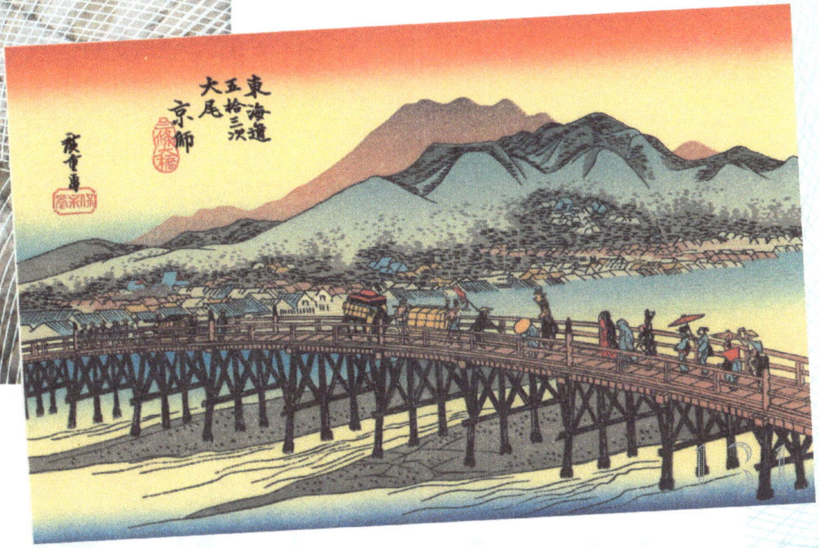
東海道
五拾三次
大尾
京師
廣重画

Out at night and a view of the lake.

132

Looking pretty suave outside the venue.

29 NOVEMBER PRAÇA DA APOTEOSE, RIO DE JANEIRO, BRAZIL 30 NOVEMBER PISTA DE ATLETISMO, SAO PAULO, BRA

4 DECEMBER OBRAS, BUENOS AIRES, ARGENTINA 5 DECEMBER OBRAS, BUENOS AIRES, ARGENTINA

7 DECEMBER MONUMENTAL, SANTIAGO, CHILE

Souvenirs of South America: Rio, Copacabana Beach and Sao Paulo. Look closely and you'll see that Steve beat me at the go-kart races, but I beat Paul.

29 NOVEMBER APOTEOSE RIO BRA
30 N ATL
4 DI AIR
5 DI AIR
7 DECEMBER SANTIAGO, CHI

Sex Pistols

A LIBRE ACCESO

Filthy Lucre Tour '96
Santiago – Chile

GLEN MATLOCK
MUSICO
SEX PISTOLS

Passport photos: my best Warhol impression, complete with fake fur.

You want to know about the minutiae of being on tour? Well, have you ever seen that film *Lost In Translation*? It was like that at times. I was on the other side of the world from my missus and my children and I couldn't have a drink. And I was jetlagged. Then again, I got to go to all these amazing places. I wasn't bored, because life's what you make it. I don't get stage fright: I get a bit keyed up before stage time, though. I think it comes when you're not sure what you're doing or why you're doing it. We were tightly rehearsed because we wanted to be good.

How did I manage jet lag? I didn't. Normally you'd have a drink and get tanked up to help you get through it, but I'm on the wagon so I couldn't do that. It was a help that Steve was also on the wagon and that Paul isn't a big drinker. A few times I felt like I wanted a drink to celebrate, but I didn't do it. Like Jimmy Greaves says, 'I'll have one tomorrow.'

The differences between life on the road in 1976 and 20 years later were legion. In 1976 we were in the back of a Transit with no windows, sitting on top of the old Electrovoice cabinets, going up the motorway. This time we flew around the world first class. I'd say it was more fun that way. That said, I thought British Airways were very stingy with their air miles. I flew around the world with them, first class, and I ended up with 1000 air miles. I couldn't believe it.

As for food, when in Rome, do what the Romans do… that's what Paul said to me. In Japan, you don't get the biggest portions, especially if you're staying in a plush hotel. I wanted something Western for a change and that's when he told me that.

Clothes? Always been important in the Pistols. After all, we were all attracted to each other by hanging out at Sex. You tend to have mates in the rag trade and you're hip to what's going on rather than just getting your clothes from Top Shop or whatever. Paul always said we were designer punks, and he was taking the mickey, but I agree with him. I don't know what it means, really. A high-end, expensive version of punk, I suppose – although it wasn't expensive if you worked there because we got a nice little discount.

Ronnie Biggs turned up in Rio, where we were playing a basketball stadium. He wanted to come into the dressing room, but he knew it was uncool to come in because John was there. I thought all that stuff was pony, too. Steve and Paul really wanted to meet him, and they were hanging on for John to go, but John knew what was going on so he didn't want to go. Ronnie was hanging about outside and he sent his mate in, this English barrow-boy type, to sound things out, and he said to me, 'Malcolm?' I thought it was funny, although it was totally the wrong thing to say, and I eventually split because I got tired of waiting to see what the outcome would be. John wasn't going to let them get away with it.

Santiago, Chile was a mad gig. It was in a basketball arena, and one end was cordoned off with a stage. Nobody was supposed to be behind the stage, but they got round there somehow. The gig was sold out but a lot more people wanted to get in: they're a bit mad in South America, and they don't really think about the fact that the money from the tickets is what pays the band. Rambo had a field day trying to get people out from behind the stage, and it got pretty lairy. Then, after the show, he ran into a monitor and cut his head. All the security were overwhelmed.

We were in the dressing room afterwards and they wouldn't let us leave. There was this strange smell, and I wanted to go out and see what it was, but they said we couldn't, even though we said, 'We're the band!' I found out later that the smell was tear gas. They'd tear-gassed everybody! But the attitude of the people there is that if you don't get tear-gassed on a Friday night, you haven't had a proper night out. And that was the last show of the Filthy Lucre tour.

The band's attitude was, 'Let's let the dust settle, and we'll see what happens next'. There had been a couple of run-ins: there was a big one in Santiago, which was nothing to do with me: it was between John and Paul and Steve.

Me, Steve and Paul went to Rio for a week, just to stay in a nice hotel and decompress. There was a big pool and it was great. I was knackered. We'd done a lot of work and a lot of travelling by then, and there had been a lot of mental stuff along the way. It felt like a success, though. I thought 'What's next?', but initially I was too tired to consider that properly.

At the airport, Steve was going to LA and Paul was off to Jamaica, I think. We all had a hug and Steve apologised for what had happened the first time around. He said, 'It wasn't us, it was Malcolm.' It was good that he said that.

At the end of the tour I had to stay out of the UK for three months so I wouldn't get clobbered with tax. I had no compunction about doing this.

I'd been in the Sex Pistols all those years ago and not earned much, so the idea of getting a big payday and giving it all away in tax didn't appeal. I still paid a fortune in tax, though, believe me. Those three months were January to March 1997, when Carol was pregnant with my second kid, so I couldn't go too far in case something happened. It's not much fun being by yourself, when you're missing your family – of course, she couldn't fly. I had a flat in Barcelona and it was kind of boring. I was trying to resurrect the solo album that I'd put out on Creation. I'd made a good record, so I was waiting for Creation to shit or get off the pot.

Getting home was a bit of an anticlimax. You come home and you think you're an all-conquering hero, but the world's moved on and you're forgotten. There was a new Labour government in May 1997 and Lady Diana died that August. It happened right opposite where my flat was. It was an exciting time, though. A lot of things changed, a lot of things stayed the same. I reconnected with a lot of old friends, like Alexander McDowell who was the very first person to book the Pistols. The thing I'm proud of is that the initial 20 or so people who were involved in the punk movement all went on to do something worthwhile in their field. They didn't all form bands, they went into fashion, graphic design, photography: it was a very go get 'em bunch of people.

The next time the Pistols did something was 2002…

BRITISH AIRWAYS
BA 079123
RL6NRY
MATLOCK
3D1F32
LONDON

We knocked a couple of ideas for new songs around when we started rehearsing in LA. I thought that I had a good track, not an entire song but a track, and Paul was interested, but John wasn't. There's a DAT knocking around with the music on it. I thought it was a real shame.

Songwriting is interesting, but tough to get right. What got me started as a music fan was the whole pirate radio movement in the 60s. Radio Caroline, London, Luxembourg… I'd hear The Who, The Rolling Stones, The Yardbirds and The Idle Race. All the songs were two and a half minutes long or they wouldn't get on the radio, and they were all about something. I heard an interview with Jacques Brel and he was asked how he wrote songs, and he said, 'I must be mad. Every good song is about somebody, so you have to narrow the whole of your life down, and the words have to rhyme, and the song has to have a rhythm, and each syllable has to have a different note, and you have to tell the story of your life – so I must be mad.' To bring that off is hard work. Inspiration comes and goes, depending on whether you're enthused about something and you've got a bee in your bonnet.

EPILOGUE

There's quite a big difference between being a teenage rebel and a middle-aged rocker. No-one in the band was a punk. Punk came later. When we formed the band we stuck our necks out: nobody was doing anything like what we were doing in this country, and if they were doing it abroad, we were very spuriously aware of it and we hadn't heard of it. You can only do that when you're a free agent and there's nothing that can hold you back. We really felt like we were on some kind of mission, and there was an excitement attached to that. In later years you have different things going on: you just get on with it.

The moment you walk on stage, it's a summation of all the things you've done before then. It's not a straight line from 1976 to 1996: you take steps away, and steps back towards, and steps away again. I think that applies to everyone. Look at The Who. Did they really want to do those old tracks at the Olympics? Maybe they did, maybe they didn't.

We're not an establishment band. It's always been a leftfield thing. We matter because we're a benchmark. As Alan McGee wrote in his review, he was standing next to Noel Gallagher of Oasis, and Noel turned to him and said, 'Blimey… we're not this good.'

We did more dates in 2003, which were essentially the same as they were on the Filthy Lucre tour but with a slightly bigger waistline. The critics were the same too: they're critics, after all. They always say we play better each time, which I don't think is necessarily the case: I think we've always played pretty well. Reunions come when the right offer is on the table. People forget that there is an element of being in a band which is just a job. Most bands that have any degree of success tour all the time and really milk it, whether it's festivals or whatever, because it's a nice little earner. It's not just something to celebrate, being in a band: it's the way you earn your money. I don't think we're any more guilty of selling out and then reforming than any other band. There are bands who do that all the time who should have split up years ago – and we're much better than all of those bands put together.

Here's the *NME* saying that the Filthy Lucre tour destroyed our credibility. The journalists who wrote things like that obviously didn't think what it means to never earn any money. They won't write about your new record, but they'll call you up and unashamedly ask you for a quote about the Clash or something. Fuck them. If we were so bad, why give us a two-page article? They're full of shit. We've done a few more tours since then, including five nights at the Brixton Academy, although we could easily have done seven, and we played the Manchester MEN Arena. They were all sold out, and people wouldn't have come if they'd thought we were crap. QED. There were good reasons to do the Pistols reunion: if it's what everyone wants, you might as well do it and get paid for it.

The Filthy Lucre tour put me back in the frame again as a songwriter, and as the guy who wrote most of the Pistols' best material. I've never claimed to be the only songwriter in the band, but I was the instigator of a lot of things. If we were all sitting around saying, 'What are we going to play now?' it would always be me who said, 'How about this? and come up with something. I felt that I'd been vindicated, and that I'd had the last laugh.

If I was careful, I would never have to work again, but that doesn't mean I'm loaded – especially when you have a couple of kids. It was an even split. Everything we earned from playing live went four ways, although there are some logistics with the merchandise because of Sid's estate, which get resolved whenever we get together.

I felt like I'd been in a kind of limbo before that point. When you've been in something as big as the Sex Pistols, anything else you do afterwards has to eclipse it. So much of success is down to timing and the right chemistry between the people: it's a very tall order to do that, but it wasn't for the want

The *NME* said that we destroyed our credibility, but they were wrong: we did what bands do, which is go out, play live, pay the bills and have fun doing it. If we were sellouts, then a thousand other bands who reformed and got paid were sellouts too. Music journalists do like to play their games.

NME REVIEWS

THIS WEEK'S GOB-LOT OF RECORDS AND LIVE REVIEWS

LIVE: Pages 39-42, SINGLES: Page 48 & 49, LONG PLAYS: Pages 50-54

Look! It really was anarchy, it really was!

LIVE
EDITED BY TED KESSLER

SHAM '96!

Cabaret in the UK: Spike Island (above), the Iggster gets Screwn Again (below) and Big Mouth Strikes again (right)

SEX PISTOLS
London Finsbury Park

LOOK OVER there – it's a small child, about 11 years old. And over there is a small boy who cannot be a day older than eight. And over there? Why, that's a six-year-old kid in a denim jacket with the word 'Buzzcocks' felt-tipped on the back. What, perchance, connects these miniature adults? Well, none of them have yet reached legal drinking age. All of them have hitched a piggyback ride to north London to see punk rock's most notorious sneermeisters play their first London show for, oooooh, 19 years. And – crucially – all of them are modelling mohicans.

That's right. Mohicans.

Bugger! The Return Of The Pistols was always bound to be a strange affair, but few punters could have been prepared for the very peculiarity of this event. As the crows feet spread, it's been a toenail-clipping two whole decades since Lord Jonathon Rotten sent the tabloids into a furious feeding frenzy by the simple virtue of singing in a band who spat, sneered, cussed and knocked out the occasional cocksure incendiary poooonk nugget.

Mucho water has passed beneath various bridges since then: they found Sid Vicious, then couldn't cling onto him; they imploded – rather brilliantly on the road in America – after one proper album and then drifted into projects which ranged from the dubious (see guitarist Steve Jones' loungings in Los Angeles) to the downright intriguing (cue John Lydon's Public Image Ltd) via lawsuits, counter lawsuits and all the other behind-the-scenes nonsense that makes rock'n'roll what it bally well is.

And, frankly, nobody gives a f— about all that right now. Because today is about the first of the last mohicans. Today is sunny. Today is balmy. Today witnesses the most comprehensive collection of tattoos, piercings, Day-Glo hair and dribbly old punkers since... since hell, no-one can actually remember. Because the original Sex Pistols line-up has dragged itself together for the 'Filthy Lucre Tour'! For lucky old us! For their lucky old wallets! And while Rotten, Jones, Glen Matlock and Paul Cook may have reformed, a multitude of mayhem-seeking sorts are wondering if the classic Bad Boys are really reformed?

There's a weird supporting cast for this potential theatre of hate – a blend of wrinkled rockers and fresh-faced thumpers. Cheery metapop manglers **3 COLOURS RED** earn an earthy (8) on the Punk Counter, thanks to guitarist Chris McCormack's classic riff-tastic legs astride posturing. That, and the fact that Chris shouts, "Alright, ma?" halfway through the set. **FLUFFY** fare rather less well on said Punk Counter, the all-girl foursome's one-dimensional riff-fondling warranting a (5), primarily because of some splendidly scuzzy bleached blonde hair and an utterly gratuitous screech of, "BOLLOCKS!!!" from singer Amanda Rootes. A Holey mess, in short.

If it comes as a mild shock that Fluffy weren't bottled off you are missing the whole point, which is that when punks reach a certain age they only throw their drinks at bands they respect. So it's an earnest (8) for old hands **STIFF LITTLE FINGERS** who cause the skies to darken with spiralling lager cartons the second they launch into opener 'Suspect Device', and who magnificently overcome the traumas inherent in wearing white footwear (Oi! Stiffies! No!). 'Alternative Ulster''s good, too.

No such Old School familiarity with **60FT DOLLS**, who bemuse the majority with their raucous booze'n'blues stint. Still, they deserve a steamy (7) on the Punk Counter for singer Richard Parfitt yapping: "You all think you're punk rock, don't you? You're not! You're a bunch of wussies! We're not scared of you – we're Welsh!" And quite mad, obviously.

THE BUZZCOCKS earn an easy (8) for the classic '70s glass-hurling likes of 'Harmony In My Head' and 'Orgasm Addict' and the fact that Pete Shelley has finally abandoned The Worst Toupee In Rock. **SKUNK ANANSIE** get a measly (3) because, politico-mungous attitude or not, 'Charity' swindles the more mature elements of the crowd into singing along – to the *slow* bits. Oh, and the Skunks' next gig is with Bon Bugger-A-Badger Jovi.

THE WILDHEARTS warrant a smooth (7) for shouting everyone into some sort of party mode, for playing rawk in the way that your psychotic granddad would appreciate and for the quote of the day from the recently-shorn Ginger: "Throwing bottles onto the stage?" he tuts. "Haven't you heard of recycling?" And there would have been a naughty (9) for **IGGY POP**, simply because he is the one artist of the day brave enough to attempt fornication with a Marshall stack, but then the Iggster blows it with a wretched 'Search And Destroy' and a karaoke-bungous 'Louie Louie'. (5) then.

And the **SEX PISTOLS**? Slap Mother Earth on the rump with a stick of celery, what the gadzooks is going on here!? After a high octane cocktail of mid-'70s sopoforicity on the DJ front, les Pistoles finally burst through a giant tabloid mock-up covering the stage. Actually, they don't so much burst as stumble, but that's not the point. The point is that no-one knows what the bloody point is. Which means that the Sex Pistols – well versed as they are in the art of being crafty little gits – can do whatever they choose. Which they do rather astutely.

"Fank you for coming to our little f—ing party!" crows Rotten/Lydon as they launch into 'Bodies' and several thousand people suddenly twig that, yes, 'It' is actually happening as the Sex Pistols balance on the precipice of an hour of snide comments, swaggering memories and still-snotty punk anthems.

They play everything, basically. That they are going to becomes screamingly apparent when they stoop low enough to trundle through their ever-hapless cover of The Monkees' 'Stepping Stone'. But that stoop apart, the Pistols do what the Pistols presumably used to do very scrappily in punk toilets in '76 extremely well on a huge stage in '96. We get 'Submission'. We get 'EMI'. We get 'Holiday In The Sun', 'Pretty Vacant' and a smashing communal singalong for 'Anarchy In The UK'. We get a crispy, sophisticated, clean-as-a-monk's-whistle sound, we get called "Tossers!"... we even get Stuart Pearce and Gareth Southgate from the England footie team introducing the bloody band. Because this, more than anything else, is desperately fine cabaret.

Johnny is in typically Rottenesque form: "Any journalists out there?" he wails at one point; "Fat, 40 and back!" he chants at another; "We're the Pistols! No-one likes us, we don't care!" he sings at yet another. Jones is in good form, as well. "Who wants a good shag?" he belches. Take care, kids – this man appears to be wearing gold lamé trousers.

And that, amazingly considering all the fuss, is it. Bung in 'God Save The Queen', a final encore of 'No Fun' and whatever else is lying around 'Never Mind The Bollocks', give it a moderately dynamic '90s twist and *voilà* The Sex Pistols have smashed any ounce of credibility, radicalism or originality they ever had within the space of 60 very silly, extremely entertaining minutes. We'd say that it made them mere mortals, but Sidney has already made that ragingly apparent.

Ultimately, we didn't know what the hell to expect. And yet, ultimately we got precisely what we expected. Funny, that.

Small children with mohicans for goalposts? Oh go away...

Simon Williams

of trying. I've never been a slacker: I've done loads of things which would have done better if they hadn't been measured against the Sex Pistols. It's a double-edged sword.

On stage we were a real band: a well-oiled machine. We'd have a chat and a laugh about the gigs afterwards: we'd say 'Did you see that bloke in the crowd?' We even talked about writing new material, but John didn't want to rise to the occasion. I had some ideas, and Chris Thomas said 'If you put a decent set of lyrics to this music, you'll have a number one' but John didn't want to do it. It was a bit like Pink Floyd, with a riff that I reappropriated from 'Interstellar Overdrive', but John thought it sounded too much like the Sex Pistols!

I suppose I've had a unique career, but there's that famous quote from Keith Richards, isn't there? They asked him if he led a normal life and he said 'Don't ask me mate, I've been a rock star for the past 40 years!' It's just par for the course for what you're doing. I'm not being big-headed: it's the way it is. I've done big shows with other people: I did some major gigs with Iggy Pop, for example, which was similar. The playing is always the same. No matter how tired or jetlagged you are, as soon as you get on stage and you hear people screaming, it drives you wild and you get into it.

The thing about the Pistols is that we have something in common that no other four people in the world have, which is that when we get together we're the Sex Pistols – regardless of what everybody is individually. It's quite an achievement to know that no matter how you get on or don't get on, nobody's ever going to take that away. John once put it well when he said, 'While the Sex Pistols will never be the best of friends, we will always be far from enemies' which I think put it rather well. There is mutual respect between us.

I'm proud of the Sex Pistols. How could I not be? Mine are good songs, most of them. It's far too late to write new Pistols songs now. I'm not interested in doing it. I just don't think it's going to happen, but the moment was right back then. It would have been a challenge. There was so much uncertainty: I've come to accept it. When you're in a band like the Pistols, with lots of people involved who may or may not want things to happen, you can't be thinking 'It's got to happen or I'll die!': you've got to be a bit more realistic than that. I could say to John, 'Oh please, come on' but I don't want to be that guy. I feel that people understand a bit more than they used to that I was the guy behind some of the band's best songs. When we went out on tour, people understood that, and remembered it for a while afterwards, but then it dissipated a bit until the next time we went out. It's a funny thing, in the light of the fact that the Queen's just had her diamond jubilee. Every time she has one of those, journalists come out of the woodwork and ask us the same questions. It never seems to go away.

The Pistols is both a blessing and a burden: it depends what you're doing at the time. It's great when we're out there being the Pistols and you're getting paid, but between those times it's hard because it doesn't reflect what you're doing then. I really don't want to live in the past, but it feels as though I'm being forced to. That's a conflict, because I feel that I'm a pretty good songwriter. But you have to go out and play the Pistols gigs, because that's what people want and it's what they're prepared to pay for. You've still got to earn a living.

When we go out as the Pistols, we're pretty damn good. John is fantastic on stage. He's hard work, but he's fantastic. Paul is still a good drummer. Steve has still got that great guitar sound. And I'm no slouch on the bass. We all learned to play together so we've all got the chemistry, regardless of any arguments that we've had in the past. We get in the room, plug in and start playing, we're the Sex Pistols.

What's my legacy? Some top, toe-tapping tunes. The Sex Pistols weren't punks: we were the Sex Pistols. Punk came afterwards.

If I spent my life waiting for the Pistols to reform, it would be a long and tedious life, and there are plenty of other things to do. Sometimes I do things because they're a nice little earner, sometimes I do things because they're fun. In recent times I've played with my all-time favourite band, the Faces; I've helped Primal Scream out; I've toured with my own band; and I've done sessions for various different people. Some of these projects are good, some are harebrained, some I do to keep my hand in, some I do for love. It's all part of life. I've been there, done that, and if the opportunity came I'd do it all again.

www.ingramcontent.com/pod-product-compliance
Lightning Source LLC
Chambersburg PA
CBHW041539220426
43663CB00003B/83